LOVE TO JOURNAL

ROOT CHAKRA

JOURNALING THROUGH THE CHAKRAS

Dale Darley

Copyright © 2020 by Dale Darley.

All rights reserved. No part of this publication may be reproduced, distributed or transmitted in any form or by any means, without prior written permission.

Love To Journal – Root Chakra – Journaling Through The Chakras
ISBN: 9798557655026

DEDICATION

Love To journal is dedicated to mum, dad (RIP), Ferdy Dog (RIP), Marley Moo and Angel. To all the people I meet randomly, thank you for having faith and putting pen to paper. It is also dedicated to you, who brave beyond words as you step into the world of journaling and make incredible discoveries about who you are.

TABLE OF CONTENTS

Welcome to the magic of word alchemy	1
Energy and your chakras	15
The Venus gateway	31
Starting to journal and write	41
Writing from the heart	45
The alchemy of the breath and meditation	51
Journaling magic	65
Daily magic	79
Journaling ideas and prompts	87
Mandalas	93
Affirmations	99
Gratitude	111
Roots and foundations journaling prompts	125
Timelines and turning points	133
Roots and feeling safe	139
Roots and trust	143
Roots and belonging	149
Roots and home	155
Roots and your family	161
Roots and abundance	165

Roots and prosperity	171
Roots and money	177
Roots and hydration	185
Roots and being nourished	189
Roots and balance	195
Roots and fear	199
Roots and letting go	211
The roots of your successful life	219
Prescription for healthy roots	223
Reflective practice and reflection	229
Learn more about Dale	237

Check out your books resources on the last page of the book.

I wish I could show you when you are lonely or in darkness, the astonishing light of your own being.
Hafiz of Shiraz

Welcome to the magic of word alchemy

The more I tune into the alchemy of words the more magical life becomes

This Love To Journal book has been designed to support you in creating a life that you love, to find clarity, purpose and meaning. Every day is an opportunity to get to know you better. You have the power to create the life you desire, discover your magic and connect to your divine inner wisdom, and this book will help you to do that.

This is a book and a course in a book which has been designed to support healthy roots and foundations. These are important because when you create healthy roots and root chakra, you are designing a powerful support system to live your life from.

This book is full of wonderful activities to support your journaling practice. You will find ideas for journaling magic, mandalas, affirmations, gratitude, and journaling prompts. *Get yourself a journal to use with this book and course.* Keep this by your bed. Your role is to dive in explore and enjoy the process. The book has been designed to guide you gently into your practice. When you get to the gratitude section, you are ready to start practising gratitude. As you begin your gratitude practice, start the root chakra journaling prompts. There are no rules. You do not have to journal daily, however, getting into a routine will help you to form a habit and reap the benefits of manifesting magic in your life.

Word Alchemy

Everything lives within us in stories. The stories we tell ourselves and others. We often fear what is within us. We fear our greatness and magnificence. Word alchemy gives you access to who you are now and who you are becoming, and what is possible for you and your unfolding future.

Word Alchemy is a tool that reveals the energy of your words, opens up your divine inner wisdom and reveals the whispers of your soul. It combines the delicious world of words and no words to get to the heart of what you want and need to express. Through word alchemy, you have the power to manifest magic and create change.

It is a portal to enquiry and curiosity and a lens through which you can view your words. It is not only about writing; instead, it provides a framework for being, living, falling in love with yourself and creating a wonder-filled life of magic.

Some people journal, some practice breathing, meditation, colouring mandalas, reflective practice, creative life writing, art journaling, find inspiration with oracle cards, and some use their connection with spirit to guide them. With word alchemy, you will bring these concepts together, so that when the words make their way to your journal, they are the words of your soul.

Within this process, you will start to notice your language, how you speak to yourself and others, your perception of words and their meaning. Not only that there is intuition, imagination and energy. The overall purpose of your word alchemy practice is to manifest magic in your life.

You will also find mandalas dotted around the book, these are designed for you to pause for thought. Read the affirmation and use this for reflection as you go about your day. Get out your colouring crayons, colour and ponder.

Journaling

Journaling is at the heart of word alchemy. This is where you capture the words your heart and soul want you to know and where you can pick up the vibration and essence of your language. Your journal is the container of your wisdom.

But first, let's look at what this journaling malarkey is all about. You may have picked this up because you or someone said you should journal. Ouch, I hate the should word. When I hear it, I rebel and do the opposite. So first things first get rid of the should and ought's and start to reflect on why you might want to journal. When I journal it's not always fun and light, but once I reflect and get my amazing aha's that's when the fun comes, and I realise that change and how I feel is in my hands. Doh!

I have been journaling for years and years. It's hard for me to remember when I started, but I do remember that it was a horrible time for me, and I felt a massive urge to write out my feelings. I didn't know anyone who journaled, nor did I have any books, I just sensed that this would make a difference to my life and it did.

In January 2018, my spine fractured. It hurt like hell, and I was terrified. My mum had Osteoporosis and five fractures, I'd witnessed her journey and knew she was in daily pain. Was this I wondered the end of my life? It felt like it. I called my health company, who said to call an ambulance. No way I heard myself saying through the tears – they are for sick people.

Friends helped me to get to the doctors and get x-rays. Every day was scarier and scarier, I wanted off the planet. After four days of taking pain killers and staring at the ceiling, I started a new healing journal. I found a pretty journal that I had been saving for a rainy day.

The good news was that I knew the benefits of journaling, reflecting, colouring mandalas, gratitude, affirmations, breathwork, and manifesting magic. The bad news was that I had other complications which meant that there was a lot of other healing that needed to take place.

I started to scribble how I felt. Screaming at my journal, I vented and spewed my anger all over the paper. I saw a specialist who told me that she wouldn't support a natural approach to healing and that I would die unless I took her drugs. I threw her prescription in the bin, cried and cried, scribbled more and then I decided that this journal would save my life. Bringing her to mind, I wrote 'I have healed, healthy bones'. And that's when it all changed.

What I also knew was that this was my soul calling me to heal the foundation of who I was. To reconnect to Mother Earth, to stay grounded, so that I could live in love rather than fear. My journal supported the rebuilding of the bones of who I am.

The power of writing

Writing is incredibly powerful. The act of writing allows your subconscious thoughts to flow. Then upon reflection, you begin to see, sense, patterns, ways through your problems and onto solutions, ideas and inspiration. You will start to get incredible insights, and if you choose, you can make some significant changes based on what you learn. When you write, you are writing for you and only you. Writing will set you free. Every word that hits the page is a little part of you.

Think about this, if you write about your fears they are almost certainly halved as you share the energy of that vibration with the page and therefore start to dissipate that feeling. When you write about overcoming difficult obstacles, you are sharing hope with your heart. When you write about success and celebration, you have a friend to share that with.

Benefits of journaling

Journaling has saved my life on many occasions, which all sounds very dramatic. I attribute the power of journaling to helping me to become who I am today.

Journaling and your physical health

Your health is your wealth. This has been the driving force for my life. Journaling has proven time and again to help fight stress (and anxiety). Stress is one of the worst things for our health. It affects all aspects of our life, including our diet, sleep and mood.

On top of that, it releases damaging hormones into our body. Reducing stress is often the trigger to a whole host of health benefits. As a stress relief tool, journaling can actually boost your physical health and well being. People who journal:

- Have a better immune system

- Tend to want to explore natural treatments and are big fans of self-care
- Often heal quicker

This is because it all goes back to the stress component. The very act of writing about things you are connected to emotionally activates certain areas in your brain. When these areas are activated, you can more efficiently process what life throws at you. Although I like to believe that life happens for me and not to me and that there are lessons and gifts in everything.

Journaling supports your mood and enables you to function cognitively at a higher level. All of which helps you come up with creative solutions to any potential problems or stressors in your life. In short, journaling gives some of the benefits you'd get if you were ranting to your best friend – not that you would do that (too often) – would you?

As I said, earlier, people who journal are less stressed, have better immune systems, heal faster, and tend to enjoy a better quality of life. Nowhere is this more evident than in people who are going through serious medical issues such as in my case, healing fractures from Osteoporosis a few years ago. Not all the benefit is from mere stress reduction, though. Journaling has been proven to raise the quality of life – it did mine and continues to do so. Those who journal while dealing with a severe medical condition do better in accepting their diagnosis, processing everything going along with it and looking for ways to support their healing. In my experience, I have seen people with illness, fare far better in treatment (natural or otherwise) than those who never journal.

You are better able to manage your emotions

Emotions are fundamental to human life, they are what keep us safe and help us to experience life. However, they are often poorly understood. A lot of research has gone into defining emotions, what they mean, how we experience the intensity of them and what they mean to us. The fascinating thing about feelings is that what we experience will differ from how others experience the same emotions. So, my experience of anger will be different from yours. You may fly into a rage, where I will only feel annoyance – yet we both describe it as anger.

One issue with emotions is the ability to really feel each part of it, understanding what that emotion means to you, the sensations you have inside your body and the thoughts that run through your mind. The more you can observe these and understand them, the more you can use these emotions for your benefit. A great way to notice your feelings is to stop regularly, enter the space within and note what you are feeling, in this way, you can learn what they mean to you. Don't judge them as bad or good. Just note them. Writing these in your journal will help you to process and understand them. Also, noticing how other people behave can be very illuminating and improve your understanding of self. Your journal can help you healthily work through emotions. You will be able to reframe them and refocus more productively. When you stop during the day, ask yourself:

- What your current state of mind is
- Ask yourself what your most dominant emotion is
- Note the intensity, e.g. Fear – fearful to terrified
- Make a note of anything else that seems relevant, like the trigger, who you were with, the environment and what was happening at the time

Reframing
Reframing is the way that you choose to see something from another perspective. In your journal, you can go on an adventure and explore the root of any triggers, emotions, thoughts, beliefs and behaviours. When you find the memory, make a conscious choice to see the past in a new way. I look at the past with gratitude and appreciation, which enables me to see the lessons, gifts and benefits. A simple way to reframe is to change; I can't into I can.

The you now perspective
Your journal enables you to ask questions, be curious and explore your past from the you now perspective. The emotions that you once experienced will now feel different. This will help you to understand yourself and others better. In this way, you can use your journal to scramble the script and tell a new story. When you do this, you can give them a better meaning and learn more about how to manage them in the present. This provides wonderful opportunities for growth and the future you.

Taking responsibility
When you see your stories in black and white, please be kind and compassionate towards yourself. Your journal is not a place for judgements. Take the stand of this has happened for me (to learn and grow) and not to me. By being responsible for your emotions and embracing what you learn over time, you will see your transformation.

Being emotionally intelligent

Emotional intelligence is about better understanding yourself and your emotions while understanding others, and their feelings. Daniel Goleman from his 1995 book, Emotional Intelligence suggests the following model for managing your emotions.

- Knowing your emotions
- Managing your own emotions
- Motivating yourself
- Recognising and understanding other people's emotions
- Managing relationships, i.e., managing the emotions of others

Journaling enables you to see patterns and pictures in how you manage your emotions and how you interact with others. Also, you can practice reframing your emotions and holding assertive conversations in your journal before having to face anyone in the flesh. All of which will improve your emotional intelligence.

Goals, dreams and desires

Journaling can help you achieve your goals, dreams and desires because it will force you to think about them, consider the why and how, and delve deeper into the situation so that you can examine all sides of it.

It encourages you to write down your goals, dreams and desires

When I start a journal, I reframe and review my goals, dreams and desires. Whether you write them down on paper or you use technology to get it all down doesn't matter. Although I am biased and believe that journaling is more effective because of the powerful connection between the paper and our brain. Once they're written, they are ready to tackle. I start with what I call a bucket list for my soul. This lets me get everything out that I want. My big life dream gets turned into a goal, and other smaller goals fall out of this.

It makes you consider why and how

As you write in your journal, you'll be forced to face the why and how of your goals. This is especially true if you write them down and use your journal to create a focus. I sort my bucket list and goals into focus areas and use these to create daily aligned and inspired actions.

It enables you to examine the blocks and resistance

When you are focused on goals, in your journal, you'll also be able to (and want to) explore blocks and resistance coming your way. It helps you avoid roadblocks in advance and creates a space for opportunities.

It makes you develop steps for success based on your goals

When you see it written down, you'll become very aware of what to put into in a plan, and what tasks go into your calendar (to-do list) for scheduling.

It helps you improve goal and intention setting

Each time you set intentions (present moment) and intentionally set goals (future-focussed) or write about your dreams and desires, you can define the steps you need to achieve them (a plan with daily aligned and inspired actions). When you actually do them, you are setting yourself up to improving your life and the direction you want to go in.

It provides accountability

Even if no one else is reading your journal, a private journal can help you become accountable to yourself and your goals. By writing down your daily actions, you will start to become accountable, and you will enjoy being able to write your success in the back of your journal. That is, of course, if you have actually carried out your action list.

It provides a permanent record

Having a permanent record of the things you've done in your life, whether it's personal or work, is a beautiful thing. Hardly anyone has a perfect memory, so the wisdom you get from reflecting on how far you have travelled is priceless.

It may be inspirational

Depending on the journal, you might even be able to take the information and insights gained and turn them into something like a book, blog or course to inspire others.

Journaling is an excellent way to work toward achieving all your goals, dreams and desires. It will even help you make better goals and set clearer intentions because the process of writing in your journal and reflecting will enable you to see the patterns and pictures of your life. This may help to 'save' your life, career or business as you will be able to see what works, and what doesn't from the feedback and reflections in your journal. You'll know when to change direction and where to place your focus.

You can express yourself freely

Being able to put into words how you perceive and experience the world is a feeling like no other. The very act of doing so provides you with a sense of satisfaction. After all, these are your impressions that your unique voice wants to express. Expressing yourself through writing is also healing. This is where you can begin to find your voice, step into your personal power, reclaim your confidence and become more assertive.

Your creativity is ignited

The more you write, the more you'll see how things fit together. You will start to see patterns and pictures and get wonderful aha moments. When you begin your exploration with a "what if..." or 'I wonder' you will make big creative leaps, leading you into fresh, new territory waiting to be explored. Encouraging your creativity to come out to play is invaluable in life and in business. Some of my best ideas have shown up when I am more relaxed with my pen poised.

You make sense of the order of things

Writing things down helps you to easily see what you need to do and how to go about doing it. Again this slowing yourself down to check that all of the steps make sense. Of course, it can be a little frustrating when you have scribbled all of the steps down to find that you have missed some vital parts. My journal is full of ideas and scribbles that just get more and more clarity as I write and reflect.

Your learning is cemented

I love the way that writing things down cements your learning. There is a connection between your hand, brain and the paper that differs to how you might write on a computer. I have personally found that I remember more when I handwrite, and I have a deeper emotional connection. Handwriting will slow you down so that you take the time to learn rather than speeding along at a rate of knots, just to get the information down. Even though it can seem longer than typing, you really will retain more for longer.

Your writing improves

The daily act of writing improves your connection with words and language. I've noticed that the way that I express myself in my journal has changed over time. I have been able to explore how to use new words. The exploration of different words in my journal means that I have a safe space away from judgement to take risks with my writing. Daily journaling trains the writing muscle and keeps it fit. Much needed when you are required to use words in all aspects of your life.

Your personal stories are captured

If you want to write your story, this is a great place to start. Your journal becomes a record of your life. No one else is experiencing the world in the same way you are. Your impressions, the way that you live your life have importance. In your journal, you preserve what it means to be you, here in this moment for your future self—and even generations to come. When you have been able to express your voice and discover how to create a life of meaning and purpose, you will potentially want to inspire others to do the same. Journaling is a stepping stone to becoming a writer, ready to stretch your wings and fly into the world of stories, blogs and books if you so desire.

Other benefits

I started saying that journaling saved my life, so I will close with other benefits that will continue to support you to find clarity, meaning and purpose.

Because your journal is private, you can: -

- Release unhelpful thoughts and learn to let go
- Gain a sense of perspective and control
- Store and analyse your dreams
- Become a catalyst for change

You will start to: -

- Understand who you are, what you want, and how to get it
- Find new ways to tackle old behaviours, issues or problems
- Unwind and relax
- Communicate with others better
- Create positive intentions and affirmations
- Discover a pathway to self-awareness that provides insights, upon which you can act and create change
- Find creative solutions to problems and challenges
- Design goals that feed your soul
- Discover memories that will support your healing and learning
- Find clarity, purpose and meaning

In the end, it's impossible to deny the benefits that come from journaling. With so many reasons to journal, the only question remaining at this point is how to go about getting started.

Journal it: Right now is an excellent opportunity to get yourself comfy, grab a cup of tea and put pen to paper to explore. Ask a question you want answering. Colour in a mandala (you can read about the benefits later) – let your mind go. In the spaces, the answers will come. Don't worry about what you write – just write. All you have to do right now is to trust that an awesome process is about to unfold. When you have written. Leave it and when you reflect on what you have written, ask what aha's do you get?

The ache for home lives in all of us, the safe place where we can go as we are and not be questioned.
Maya Angelou

Energy and your chakras

Connect and be one with the power of your inner energy.

Energy has been described by many different cultures, such as Chi, Ki and Prana, a life-force. Scientists describe it in another way more practical way, measuring ions and atoms. Energy for me is everywhere and everything. Our food, the air that we breathe and every cell in your body has an energetic impulse. As you sit quietly and consider you - you are using and harnessing energy. Breathing circulates and connects your energy, and without breath, you are dead. Healers harness energy to heal. People with passion bring energy into everything that they do, and this energy creates action. To create change, you need energy.

Journaling brings the energy of your heart and soul to the paper. The more you journal, the more you will form good energy habits. The habits you form consume large quantities of energy. If you cultivate good habits that energy will stay healthy and provide a powerhouse for your new life. Your journaling will connect you to the data contained within your chakras. I call this everywhere energy the energy superhighway. Practising journaling, gratitude, affirmations and visualisation while being connected with your chakras will raise your vibration, help to open and balance your chakras as a result. This practice can attract more abundance, happiness, health, peace, love, meaningful relationships, and other positive attributes into your life.

What are chakras?

The chakras are **energy points or centres** in our bodies in and out of which energy flows. In Sanskrit chakra means wheel so you could imagine them to be spinning wheels or vortexes of energy. Just as you have memories stored in your brain, your chakras are mini data centres where everything that has happened to you is stored. Each centre houses specific experiences. How cool is that to have your own mini you library stored in areas of your body? I also believe that they hold keys to our future selves too.

Just as we have a physical body, chakras can be likened to our spiritual body. Each one acts like a window to the soul and will feed information back to you about the state of your health and life. The health and energetic vibration of each chakra is influenced by the energies that surround you and the energy you project from your thoughts and feelings. This shows up in how you feel and experience life.

Each chakra has a colour that resonates with a specific frequency on the colour spectrum. If you know the colours of the rainbow, you will know the colours of the chakras:

- Root - Red
- Sacral - Orange
- Solar plexus - Yellow
- Heart - Green
- Throat - Blue
- Third eye (Brow) - Indigo
- Crown - Violet (white/gold)

Because light affects every living cell, the colours of the chakra system affect us emotionally, physically, mentally, and spiritually. Because of this, we can use colour frequencies to balance and rejuvenate our chakras. However, although these are the colours that we commonly use, you may find as you connect to your chakras and meditate on them another colour will appear. That is the colour that will bring healing right now. The important thing is to not be wed to what the colour should be, simply trust that the colour that you see, or sense is your colour.

The chakras are also classified by male or female energies:

- Masculine chakras (the odd chakras) - 1st chakra: root chakra / 3rd chakra: solar plexus chakra / 5th chakra: throat chakra
- Feminine chakras (the even chakras) - 2nd chakra: sacral chakra / 4th chakra: heart chakra / 6th chakra: third eye chakra

Why is it important to know about the chakras?

The chakras are fascinating and provide a framework for understanding who you are, what you want and how to become the person you want to be. This basic overview is to give you a feel for the chakras and what is available to you. Each chakra has several themes and a specific emotion. By taking the time to work with each chakra and the themes while understanding the emotions, you will start to see where you are in or out of balance. Then you can make conscious choices to change and enjoy life more.

In simple terms, the chakra system is an incredible diagnostic and self-help tool. For our bodies to function optimally, all of our seven chakras need to be balanced. This means that your vital energy is flowing smoothly through your body. If one of the energy centres is not functioning at it's best, then the others won't work as well as they should. Some of them can be overactive, and some of them can be underactive, just as say your thyroid might be one or the other. This is something you will pick up over time as you work with them. It is better to learn your energy patterns than rely on what others say – although it can be useful in some situations to read up about each of these as a guide.

I believe that if you understand the principals of the chakras, the better able you will be able to self-diagnose imbalances and be able to take the necessary action for realignment on your own. You may find it difficult to keep them balanced as you rush around and forget to take time out to do some simple daily balancing. It's like remembering to drink water, the more you do it, the better you will feel.

By learning about and tuning in with the seven major chakras, you can become more aware of the natural energy cycles of your body. Which has to be a good thing. You will also pick up information about your experiences which will help you to heal and grow. You can then look at your experiences from a place of gratitude, love, learning and appreciation.

An overview of your chakras

Root – Foundations and the right to be here

The root chakra is located at the base of the spine at the tailbone in the back, and the pubic bone in front. The right of this chakra is simply to be here. It is the first of our three physical chakras.

Colour red. Element earth. Taurus, Virgo and Capricorn are earth element signs. Planet – Saturn. The right to be here. Emotion – fear. Endocrine gland - Gonads. Spine - The coccyx (tailbone). Age 0-7

Needs

The root chakra is about your needs for survival, security, safety, trust, belonging, health and wellbeing, family, past life issues home and money. This is where you will want to create a home, not only to live in but your home on earth and the home you make in your body. When we think of the root chakra, we think of grounding and connecting with Mother Earth. Which is where we get the beautifully vibrant, abundant earth colours of red, brown and black. This chakra supports the upward flow of energy from Mother Earth.

Balanced

When balanced, you feel grounded in the present and able to confidently release the fears that hold you back from growing into who you want to become. You will feel safe and secure in yourself, you'll trust yourself and the decisions you make. Home feels welcoming and cosy, you feel like you belong. You get enormous satisfaction from being in nature and breathing in fresh air. Balancing this chakra lays the foundations for the chakras above it.

Manifesting

When you have healthy roots and foundations, you have a great base from which to manifest what you want in life. You will trust that abundance is available to you and feel at home asking for what you want.

Root chakra - Fear

This chakra is blocked by fear which closes down our right to be here. When you identity fear and the roots of it, you will begin to understand how you can start to eliminate it. Ask yourself what you are afraid of the most, and what is the worst that can happen? Who will you be when you feel safe and secure? When you move along the fear-love spectrum towards love, you will find that you will release more fear because you cannot hold onto both at once.

Sacral – Creativity and the right to feel

This chakra is located two inches below the navel and is rooted in the spine. The right of this chakra is the right to feel, which means feeling emotionally connected to yourself and to others around you.

Colour orange. Element - water. Cancer, Scorpio and Pisces are water signs. Planet – Jupiter. The right to feel. Emotion – guilt. Endocrine gland – Pancreas. Spine – L3 to L5. Age 8-14

Needs

This is about your needs around sexuality, creativity, emotions, nourishing yourself, connection with your inner child, pleasure, play, self-expression, nurturing intuition, Intimacy and the roots of self-esteem. So often this is where you might stuff down your emotions which can create problems later in life. And also where you might lose your creative side as you try to conform with what others expect of you. At this chakra, this is where you will want to invite your inner child to come out to play.

Balanced

When this chakra is in balance, it is easier to be in touch with your emotions and to more fully express your feelings in the world. You feel creative and start to feel confident in your creativity, have a sense of self-esteem, maintain good health practices, are connected to good emotional responses, are emotionally intelligent and enjoy connection and contact with others. When I think of this chakra, I also think of pleasure, play and joy, this is where your inner child has the most fun. Think of things that you can do like sing, dance and paint.

Manifesting

When it comes to manifesting, you will be able to use your creativity and to uncover what you want, and you will know what it feels like when you have it.

Sacral Chakra - Guilt

This Chakra is blocked by guilt which closes down our right to feel. To support this chakra, learn to accept that these things happened, let go and forgive yourself. Remember we are here to learn and without lessons, how will we ever learn? Ask what do you blame yourself for? Do you feel that you have let somebody down? Did you hurt someone close to you? Do you feel like you failed your parents or your partner? Who will you be when you no longer feel guilt for things you perhaps don't need to. Forgiving yourself and others is a powerful way to release guilt and live a life you deserve. Never feel guilty for being honest about how you feel, and never apologise for being you.

Solar Plexus – Identity and the right to act

This chakra is located two inches below the breastbone behind the stomach, near your belly button. The right at this chakra is the right to act.

Colour yellow. Element - fire. Aries, Leo, and Sagittarius are fire element signs. Planet – Mars. The right to act. Emotion – shame. Endocrine gland – Adrenals. Spine – L2 to T5. Age 15-21

Needs

This chakra is about personal power, confidence, assertiveness, personal boundaries, personal leadership, self-control, and self-esteem. Remember when as a child or young person, you wanted to express your individuality and how that might have felt, this is where you first experienced exerting your will and the right to be you. This chakra right means acting with confidence, honouring your personal values, and bravely taking steps towards goals and intentions.

As your centre of personal power, self-image and self-esteem, this is a beautiful space to allow the warrior or goddess inside of you to shine. At this chakra, you are called to listen to your intuition (gut feelings) rather than listening to outside voices and using your will to achieve what you desire. It's also about taking responsibility for choosing how you want to live your life.

Balanced

When this chakra is balanced, you feel confident in who you are, assertive and motivated. You listen to your gut feelings and trust who you are becoming. You set clear goals, and intentions, you move confidently forward to achieve them. You assert your will in a healthy way because you value your relationship with yourself and others.

Manifesting

In terms of manifesting what you want, this chakra is about who you will become when you have what you want.

Solar plexus chakra - Shame

Your solar plexus chakra is blocked by shame. This shame closes down your connection to your right to act and take action. Releasing shame creates a balanced third chakra which allows self-esteem and self-worth to grow. Ask yourself what you are ashamed of? Often we have shame related to our bodies, eating habits, abilities, sex and things we have done, but would rather forget. When you get caught up in this, you will feel unworthy and unloved. The way to heal this chakra and release shame is to unconditionally accept and believe in yourself. When you start choosing you, this creates the foundations for self-love to grow.

Heart – Love and the right to love and be loved

This chakra is located behind the breastbone in front and on the spine between the shoulder blades in back. This is about your right to love and be loved.

Colours green or pink. Element - air. Gemini, Libra and Aquarius are air element signs. Planet – Venus. The right to love and be loved. Emotion – grief. Endocrine gland – Thymus. Spine – T4 to T2. Age 22-28.

Needs

This chakra is about love, self-love, compassion, forgiveness, understanding, generosity, empathy, kindness and connections to other's hearts. This is the centre of love and is connected to your relationships with family, lovers, friends, and animals. This is where the physical and spiritual chakras meet and is the gateway between them. As you work to heal and balance the chakras below, this enables the hurts held here to also be healed. By learning to let go of the pain and grief, you will be able to open your heart to new experiences and love.

Balanced

When this chakra is balanced, you feel open, kind, receptive, giving, forgiving, accepting, and connected in a loving way to both yourself and other people. You feel sincere gratitude and appreciation for your life. You feel the love flowing through your life, you will think about how you give and receive love. And when you feel on the same wavelength with someone, it is because you have a heart connection.

Manifesting

In terms of manifesting what you want, the gratitude and appreciation you feel here will support you to get more of what you want.

Heart chakra - Grief

The heart chakra is blocked by grief and closes down our right to love and be loved. Releasing grief creates a balanced heart, that means we can offer acceptance and compassion to others and ourselves. It is the place that allows for vulnerability and welcomes in love. Ask what you are sad about? What are your losses? Dealing with loss is a hard thing to do indeed. Consider this, love is energy, and that lost love is reborn in the form of new love. Ask yourself what the deepest, most painful loss you ever experienced is? A loss of a job/career/business? A loss of health? A loss of a friend or a loved one? The loss of love? How did you ever get over it? Are you maybe still holding on to it? Our hearts feel and experience the pain of grief and loss physically, emotionally, energetically and spiritually. It is the gateway to unconditional love within us and to others around us.

Throat – Voice and the right to speak and hear the truth

This is located in the V of the collarbone at your lower neck. The right of this chakra is to speak our truth in a way that others can listen and understand. This is the first of your spiritual chakras.

Colour blue. Element - ether. Planet – Mercury. The right to speak and hear the truth. Emotion – lies. Endocrine gland – Thyroid. Spine – T1 to C5. Age 28-34.

Needs

The throat chakra is how you communicate, listen and understand. A lot of personal transformation can occur here when you finally learn to find your voice and speak your truth. It is from here you can communicate and express your divine inner wisdom. You will find yourself being sensitive to the power of words, thinking about how you speak to yourself and others. It also influences your ability to actively listen to and hear others, which is how you create your foundation for understanding. This is the first of the spiritual chakras which opens the gateway to developing clairaudience and the other chakras.

Balanced

When this chakra is balanced, you will be able to express yourself well, communicate clearly and listen to your intuitive inner voice as well as others.

Manifesting

In terms of manifesting opening your throat and speaking your truth will enable you to express confidently what you want and who you are.

Throat chakra - Lies

The throat chakra is blocked by lies which closes down your communication centre and your right to hear and speak the truth. It is affected by the lies that we tell ourselves and lies that we tell others. By releasing any lies, you can gain perspective and clearly communicate with integrity with the world. Ask, what part about yourself are you in denial with? What lies do you tell others and yourself – and why? Who will you be when you no longer feel the need to hide behind lies? When you dare to express who you are and what you stand for the lies that you may tell or the deceptions will fall away, and you will be more honest with yourself and others.

Third Eye – Vision and the right to see

This is located above the physical eyes on the centre of the forehead. The right of this chakra is the right to see without illusions.

Colour - indigo. Element - light. Planet – Sun. The right to see. Emotion – illusion. Endocrine gland - Pituitary. Spine – C4 to C2. Age 35-41.

Needs

Your third eye chakra is about seeing differently, perception, imagination, your psychic ability, and higher intuition. It also deals with your relationship with yourself and connection to your Higher Self. It is the place of imagination, insight, visualisation, dreams, and visions. Here you will receive guidance which can be corroborated with your emotions at the sacral and gut feelings at the solar plexus. This chakra acts as our guiding light in life, giving us the ability to see solutions, be objective, and clear-headed. It is here that we bridge left and right-brained thinking and get our most significant insights. This is the second of the spiritual chakras which opens the gateway to developing clairvoyance.

Balanced

When this is balanced, you understand how things around you are working, you can solve challenges calmly, you will have clarity of vision and thought, you are imaginative and intuitive, and possess great insight. Using your intuition and imagination and can turn your ideas into brilliant visions. You will use this inner sense to ask for guidance to make the right decisions.

Manifesting

In terms of manifesting what you want, you are able to envision what it will look like when your dreams become a reality.

Third eye chakra - Illusion

This chakra deals with insight, which is blocked by illusion, and this closes down our right to see. This chakra asks us to release the illusions that hold us back from clarity and truth. When your visions are not allowed to come to fruition, then you can feel separated from all that is dear to you. It is believed that one of the biggest illusions humans have is the illusion of separation. The illusion that we are separated from the rest of the world. Because in fact, we are all one. We may not be equal, but energetically we are one. Ask why you are unable to create a vision for your life? What illusions do you put in the way of bringing your visions to life? When you dare to dream and turn these into goals, you will find that your life will change in unexpected ways.

Crown – Connection and the right to know and understand

This is located just behind the top of your skull. The right of this chakra is to know and understand.

Colour violet. Element - consciousness. Planet – Moon. The right to know. Emotion - attachment. Endocrine gland – Pineal. Spine – C1. Age 42-49.

Needs

The crown chakra connects you to your highest spiritual consciousness, the divine, expanded personal expression, purpose and having an open mind. The crown chakra focuses your attention on the spiritual side of life. It allows for your spirituality to become integrated into your physical life. The crown chakra gives you access to the divine and motivates you to seek a deeper connection to the divine. It is also knowing that the divine is in all of us. It is a place of intuitive knowledge and wisdom. Remember that the first chakra connects you to Mother Earth, this chakra connects you to the divine and when they are connected to each other create a universal pathway that supports mind, body, soul and spirit. This is the third of the spiritual chakras which opens the gateway to developing claircognisance.

Balanced

When this chakra is balanced, you feel connected to Universal consciousness, your higher-self, can see and understand the bigger picture and that there is a purpose larger than what is going on inside yourself. You will have a deeper understanding of what your life purpose it and how that brings meaning into your life.

Manifesting

In terms of manifesting, your connection with the Universe will enable you to manifest magic, and bring your dreams into consciousness.

Crown chakra - Attachment

This chakra is blocked by attachment and closes down our right to know. By releasing attachments (psychological or physical), we are able to be aware of a global or collective conscious, as well as the larger purpose. You may be feeling lost and creatively stuck as if everyone else knows what they're doing, but you don't know what to do next. Ask what you are attached to? Money, love, sex, things? How can you let these attachments go? Who will you be when you let them go? The goal is to completely surrender; letting go of anything that has a hold on you. It is said that to open this chakra, you need to let go of attachments and outdated beliefs so that you can feel a greater sense of inner peace.

Let's connect to the chakras

The first thing to do is to simply become aware of what the chakras are and where they are in your body. Place a hand on each, in turn, breathe and tune it. What do you pick up? Don't worry if nothing happens, this all comes with time. For now, tune in ask 'what do you want me to know?' Who knows what will come up…

- Rub your hands together quickly and generate some heat

- Then send roots from your feet to the heart of Mother Earth
- Breathe gently in and out through all of your chakras, out of the crown around your body, back to earth
- Do three rounds of this
- Then place your hands on either each chakra in turn or the ones you feel drawn to
- Ask conscious and open questions
- Journal what comes up and look out for information coming to you during the day

Journal it: Spend some time daily exploring your energy systems in any way that works for you. What do you pick up when you put your hands on your chakras? Ask 'what do you want me to know? Do not stop to journal each thing that you pick up. Wait until you are finished and only journal what you remember. As you go about your day, other things will come to you, record these in a notebook or in your journal later.

The chakras and your intuition

As a part of developing your intuitive abilities knowing how you receive information is key, however, you also need to balance and work with your chakras so that you as a receiving device is flowing and ready. Working with the chakras will enhance your abilities. Each chakra provides a part of the puzzle: You work on the lower chakras to help prepare you for connecting to your intuition at the upper chakras.

- Roots – When you feel safe, secure and grounded, you can explore your intuition because you know that it is safe to do so. Also, intuitive people can read other peoples' body language and are aware of their own body sensations, such as chills, tingles, etc. which are providing intuitive clues
- Sacral – At this chakra, you start to acknowledge what you are feeling. This emotional connection creatively guides you towards your answers
- Solar plexus – When you are standing in your personal power, feel confident and assertive, you will begin to trust your gut feelings and not allow your head to take over. This is the centre for clairsentience
- Heart – The heart is the gateway between the lower physical chakras and the upper spiritual ones. This is where the wisdom of your heart lives, and It is here that you will ask your heart what it thinks about your choices and decisions

- Throat – This is the centre for intuitive hearing and listening. This is when you hear words, sounds or music in the voice of your own mind. Sometimes you may hear tones or other noises. It is the centre for clairaudience
- The Third Eye – This is the centre of psychic intuition and psychic visions. This is when you see images or visions in your mind's eye, or third eye, much like a daydream. This is the centre for clairvoyance
- The Crown chakra – This chakra connects you with spirit and your higher self. This is where you have knowledge of people or events that we would not normally have knowledge about. You seem to just know the facts with a sense of certainty. Also, spirit sends messages that simply pop into your minds from out of nowhere. This is the centre for claircognisance

Meditation and being mindful helps you to focus your awareness and go within. Start each day with a meditation that connects your heart to the heart of Mother Earth and the heart of consciousness. After which you can take your awareness to each chakra and bring balance and peace to it.

You may not feel a change for a while, but be patient. It will be interesting to notice the changes to your psychic awareness.

Recognising your dominant style of sensing

How do you recognise what your preferred or dominant style of sensing is? I always start with knowing what my preferred style of ordinary communication is – visual, auditory, or kinaesthetic. When I know this, I will practice flexing my style, so that I create more self-awareness around each.

Journal it. Sit quietly now where you won't be distracted for a few minutes. Scan the area around you, taking in all details and feelings of where you are. Then close your eyes and focus on your breath. Breathe deeply and slowly as you mentally review what caught your attention when you scanned the room. Was it the sight of something, the sound of something, the feeling of something, a taste or smell perhaps you got a thought or a knowing? What did you learn? How did you receive information?

The Venus gateway

I follow my heart, and that's where I am

The Venus gateway is a portal into your inner wisdom, your chakras and is how you develop the manual of you. As you connect to the energy of the heart and travel with her, you discover what you need each day and indeed every moment. The heart is the centre of your YOUniverse. Imagine the Venus gateway with a portal at the centre which you see (sense, know, feel) yourself going through. When you get to the other side, you will receive information which will support you in making sense and find meaning in your life. When you get to the other side, become a witness to what is there. Checking in with the flow of energy is vital. When in doubt, always come back to the heart.

Venus is the planet of love, and in mythology is the goddess of love. It is appropriate that she should accompany you on your adventure and exploration. I see her as a warrior who takes no nonsense and who will always guide you in the right direction.

Your heart needs to open to enable you to grow. We are all like butterflies waking up and learning to fly. It seems that before we can grow, we have to in some way fall apart. And out of the pain, something magical happens, we wake up, and all of the pieces fit together and flow returns: We move through revolution – the fast hard lessons and evolution – the slow, sustaining growth.

When you learn to trust, it's then that your heart opens, the cage falls away, and you can feel your way around what it means to experience life. It doesn't mean that you have everything sussed and it's plain sailing. Oh no that's far too easy. It means that you are now more aware of where you find yourself, what you want to create, and who you want to be.

When the portal opens, and your heart is ready to journey, Venus guides you to the right energy centre – the one that can support you right now. Everything starts with and flows around the heart and relies on a healthy heart connection – which you create over time. The heart is your universal messaging agent. It's a checkpoint. If it's OK with the heart, it's usually OK with the Universe. When any part of your life is stuck, you ask the heart where to go for your answers. Simply ask good questions, listen, and you will know where to go next. This brings you back into balance and flow.

What is the Venus gateway?

The Venus gateway is a portal through which you can travel to discover answers within you and your chakras. It is a way to create a daily connection with your heart. I envision it as a big circle (gateway) surrounded by the colours of the chakras, set on a platform with three steps which take you into the centre of the portal and three steps that take you down to the chakra pathways.

When you step into the portal, you are immediately in its energy – which is love and the balancing energy of all seven chakras. When you step through and down to the other side, the chakra pathways are in front of you. You ask then yourself to be intuitively guided along the right path for you.

How do you use it?

You use the Venus gateway to follow your heart's guidance and intuition so that you know where next and what next? It's about keeping it simple, intuitive and heart-led. When you have stepped through the gateway, into the energy of the portal, stepped down the other side, found the right path and connected with a chakra, you then ask, what do I need to know? You can use this on waking for daily guidance or when you have a specific question. You can set your intention to follow a particular chakra pathway and investigate that one.

Set your intention

Set your intention that you are going to travel through the portal of the Venus gateway to make a discovery about what your chakras want to share with you.

Connect

Connect to your heart using the three hearts short meditation (The alchemy of the breath and meditation). Repeated in short form here for ease. Imagine that roots are growing from your feet into the heart of Mother Earth. Place your hands on your heart. Take your awareness to your heart. Take your breath from your heart down through your roots and into the heart of Mother Earth. Breathe in and out a few times. Next, take your awareness from your heart up and out through your crown chakra and connect to the heart of consciousness. Breath in and out of your heart into the heart of consciousness a few times. Then imagine that there is a golden thread connecting the heart of consciousness to your heart and the heart of Mother Earth. When you are ready, take a few deep breaths, stretch and get ready to go through the portal.

Go through the portal

See, sense or know that the Venus gateway is in front of you. Step up to the gateway, stand in the portal's energy and step down to the beginning of the chakra pathways.

Ask - where do I need to go?

When standing at the start of the pathways, ask where do you need to go and allow your intuition to guide you. The path and colour you settle on is the chakra that you need to work with. You can also do this with a pendulum and a diagram. You will be guided by your primary sense (see, sense, feel, hear or know). If you are visual you will see colours or images, you may feel or sense where to go. I, for example, see the colour and the pathway in front of me. No matter which chakra you land on explore it as it will give you clues to do with the main chakra that this book is focusing on. You can always go back to the previous chapter and read the chakra summaries.

Ask questions

Place your hands, or take your breath or senses to the chakra you have been guided to. When you are ready, you can ask your questions. Keep your questions open so that you can explore. Closed questions where you get a yes and no can also be appropriate. Notice what comes up for you. Emotions, feelings, words, images, colours, sounds, smells or perhaps nothing. Even if you sense what seems to be nothing, still say thank you. If you get nothing, be assured that you will get other messages as you go about your day.

Questions to ask

Here is a selection of questions you can ask, one of them will resonate. As you use the gateway and your chakras more, you will know how each chakra will help you to discover your answers. The question I use most is, what do I need to know?

- **Where am I?** This question asks you to take a 360-degree view of where you are. When you know this, then you can decide where next. You could also use your life focus areas to guide and support you.
- **Where have I been?** This question allows you to check what from your past you need to reflect on, that will guide you in your quest. In the chakra overview, you will see that each is developed at a certain age. How did I get here is your map and you can use it to look back on for clues and insights. In the chapter on timelines and turning points, you will be guided to explore these ages and experiences further.
- **What do I want?** This question is to help you to clear about what it is you genuinely want as a result of having your question answered and your wish granted. Remember your bucket list for the soul?
- **Where am I going?** This question is an action question. If you know where you are going, you can then ask – how will I get there?
- **How will I get there?** This question is used for you to explore how you think you might get to where you are going and what aligned actions you need to take.
- **Who am I and who am I becoming?** This question is to for you to explore who you are now and who you will become when your question has been answered.
- **What blocks are in my way?** There will always be blocks. As you clear one, another one will arise. Notice what they are and work on forgiving and letting go. See manifesting magic later.
- **What do I need to let go of?** This question asks you what stands in our way of getting what you want or going where you desire. What is standing in my way, are they:
  - Thoughts
  - Feelings
  - Emotions
  - Beliefs
  - Behaviours
- **How can I make this simple for me?** This question asks you to consider how you might be making things difficult for yourself and how to make it simpler for you.

Is there another chakra with clues?

Ask if there is another chakra that you need to communicate with. If yes, go there and ask your questions. Follow the flow of your intuition.

Patterns
Notice the patterns of where you are guided. What I mean by this is, as you are directed to one chakra, are you then also guided to one either side or somewhere else? Is there a regular pattern? If so, ask what this means for you. For example, if I am guided to the heart chakra because I am grieving a loss, I might also be directed to the throat, because there is some truth I need to hear about the loss. I may have been telling myself some lies, and I need to know the truth of the situation surrounding the loss. In addition, I may also feel guilt or blame. Notice your patterns and ask what you learn.

Say thank you and return

When you are ready and have the information you need, say thank you and come back through the portal. Before coming back through take a look around in case, there is other information, images, sounds, smells or feelings that will support you.

Journal what you learn

Grab your journal and scribble down what you learn.

Questions and affirmations
In your journal, you can also look at the chakra rights of the chakra or chakras you visited and can create a journaling question or an affirmation to take you through the day

- How would it be if I knew that I had a right to be here?
- What might happen if I spoke from my heart today?
- Who will I be if I embrace kindness today?
- How can I be kinder today?
- I am kind to myself today
- I am grounded, centred and connected to the abundance of the Universe

Messages and clues

Go about your day. In all cases, you will get messages from spirit, guides or your body about what you need to know. Notice the memories that come up. Do they relate to a particular age or time in your life? Each of the chakras develops in blocks of seven years, starting at the root with years 0-7. These memories hold clues. It's not about being in the memory, more being an observer and knowing what the memory is telling or showing you. This ability to observe will come over time. It's like unlocking a box of clues. Over time it will make sense. Writing it in your journal and putting them on your timeline will help you to get your aha's.

Actions

Follow the steps to connect with the Venus gateway and explore. Keep a record in your journal of what comes up for you and the actions you decide to take.

Journal it: Record what comes up for you. Take some time out and then come back to reflect. What do you learn?

And remember, no matter where you go, there you are.
Confucius

Starting to journal and write

Words are, of course, the most powerful drug used by mankind. Rudyard Kipling

You would think that writing in a journal should be easy. For some, that is just not the case. In this section, I offer some hints and tips which will help you to start and keep going, plus some ideas that will support your journaling and writing.

Getting into a great state

The first thing that I do is to get into the right frame of mind to start writing in my journal or for colouring in mandalas; this includes dealing with all the mundane tasks that need doing. I make sure I'm in loose clothing (often in my pyjamas as I love to write in bed), I have a cup of tea or glass of water, and I am in a warm, comfortable place. If my jaw is clenched or I feel tense in some way, I take a few moments to focus on my breathing. When I focus on my breath, I often place my hands on my heart as I believe that when we write, it comes from the heart.

Body awareness

Sit quietly for a few moments and become aware of your body, take your attention to your toes, now let your awareness move up your body through every single part. Feel which parts feel uncomfortable and which parts feel comfortable. Breathe into each uncomfortable part and let it go. You could imagine that the painful bits are a piece of newspaper, which is old news. Scrunch it up and throw it away.

Mental pictures

What mental pictures do you have now? Where are they? How far away are they from you? Are they in colour or in black-and-white? What do these pictures mean to you? How might you interpret them?

The sounds around you

As you sit quietly, what sounds do you notice? Are there sounds in the room? Can you hear sounds in the distance? Are you talking to yourself? What sort of things are you saying to yourself? What are you filtering in or out?

Balancing

You need to stand up to this one. Place your feet hip-distance apart, let your hands hang by your sides, close your eyes and feel a sense of where you are in the room. Are you leaning to one side? Are you falling forwards or backwards? How can you rebalance you? Get a sense of balance and then open your eyes.

Noticing your state of mind and emotions

Simply stop and tune in. What do you notice about your current state of mind and emotions? This is a wonderful way to notice the effects of the day, if you are journaling at night or how you feel as you start your day. If your most dominant emotion is negative, what has to happen to turn that into a positive one? Make a choice to choose a different emotion. If it is positive, what can you do to hold on to it and really enjoy it?

Gratitude

When you are feeling rubbish and think that the world is against you, write ten things you are grateful for, right at this moment. Once you start, it is quite liberating and illuminating. You could simply be grateful for your cup of tea.

Having a magical month

To make any journey a success, you need to make plans. Be prepared to create a journaling habit that works for you. This could mean spending at least 10-15 minutes each morning and the same in the evening to set up your day and to then wind down and reflect. On Sunday, reflect on your week, declutter and dump ready for the next week and at the end of the week/month spend some time reflecting.

Accountability partner

Do you have an accountability partner or group? I find that this helps me to stay on track. Who could support you? All you need is one hour each week to check with each other that everything is on track. If you do not have anyone look for a coach or mentor, who can act as your sounding board.

Name of accountability partner/coach/mentor _____

Writing from the heart

Writing became such a process of discovery that I couldn't wait to get to work in the morning: I wanted to know what I was going to say. Sharon O'Brien

By listening to your heart, you can create a pathway for your inner voice to be heard. When you listen, you can be guided, not by what's going on around you, but by your intuition. Listening to your heart and letting it speak is connecting to your inner wisdom, your spiritual self, intuition and insight. It is the part of you that truly knows you, but which may be hidden from you. When you are ungrounded and unbalanced your connection to you will waiver. It's a little like tuning into a radio station; you need to fiddle with the dial until you get a clear and strong signal.

    To get to the inner you, you need to switch off the noise in your head and feel your way through your body. Really feel into your heart space. Feeling is sometimes difficult for many who naturally live in their heads, and always question what is going on. This is something that I have struggled with, but with time and practice, it does get easier to travel inwards and see, sense, feel, and just know what is going on. Try the three hearts meditation in the alchemy of the breath chapter.

Trying to find balance in your life can be tough. Being balanced is being grounded and centred. Being grounded is about feeling physically connected to you, having a connection with the present, with the core of who you are and staying centred on what you want from your heart. When you are grounded and centred, you open to the universe and become a channel for universal energy to connect to.

Stop for a moment, put your hands on your heart and feel where you are, what do you notice? Being connected to the inner you means that you are listening in an inattentive yet focused way to what your body, heart and soul needs. When this happens, you allow yourself to become connected to everything and nothing and at the same time, becoming open to ideas, imaginations and inspiration. Being connected to the heart of you and your inner wisdom is also about accepting and loving you, warts and all. When you learn to take responsibility for you and your feelings, you gain personal power.

Writing from the heart and personal power

Personal power is about who you are in the world from the perspective of your inner world and how you trust yourself and relate to the outer world. Your personal power is connected to the solar plexus, the heart of who you are, which allows you to write from your heart space.

When you are unable to trust yourself, feel inadequate, search for external approval, unable to assert yourself and have low self-esteem, you are disconnected from your power source and your heart. Personal power is about mind, heart and your internal spirit. It is based on your attitude to life, values, thoughts, feels and beliefs. By uniting your personal power with your heart, you are connecting to self-love, purpose and meaning, which is a wonderful place to write from.

Your power is in holding yourself accountable for your choices and actions

Being grounded and centred allows you to connect with your inner wisdom, which means taking action and making choices from your heart and because you trust yourself. When you get feedback from your choices that helps you to improve what you do and how you do it.

Your power is in knowing you

When you have faith in who you are and feel grounded and connected to your heart, have meaning and purpose in your life, you have power.

Your power is in the now

Focus (in an inattentive way) on what you are doing right now, you will probably notice things which pop up and distract you. I know it happens to me. Being in the now disrupts the chaos, brings calm, focus, inner peace and contentment.

Your power is being able to let go

How many times do you have to wander off the track only to come back to what you already knew was who you are? As many times as was necessary for you to gain insights and answers. Being grounded and connected to your sense of self and your heart allows you to come back to who you are and to be able to throw off the shackles that tie you down. Imagine how it will feel to let go of what does not serve you?

Why connect to the heart of you?

Often, we are motivated by inner discontent, this turns off our antennae, and we don't hear the quiet inner voice that is guiding us. Connecting to the inner you, your heart, simply asks that you trust the process, trust you and plug back into who you are. By tuning into your inner wisdom and following your heart's guidance will help you to attract more of what you focus on. We do it because from within there is only the truth, and when we act from a place of purity, we are acting for our greater good. Your inner you reflects your core values and operating from your core values is operating from an authentic platform. In the gifts of imperfection, Brene Brown says "Authenticity is the daily practice of letting go of who we think we are supposed to be and embracing who we are."

Journal it: Bring your attention to your heart space and write freestyle for ten minutes.

Let your heart guide you into the depths of who you are

The alchemy of the breath and meditation

There is pure magic in the beauty of every breath

Trees are the lungs of the planet. Trees take carbon dioxide out of the air and replace it with oxygen. This is vital for humans, as we need oxygen in the air to breathe. Without oxygen, you won't survive. You cannot exist without your breath. Your lungs like the trees remove waste carbon dioxide from the blood and recharge it with oxygen.

Your lungs play an essential role and are responsible for supplying oxygenated blood to every organ of the body and eliminating the waste matter from the cells through expiration. The lungs inspire as you inhale and expire as you exhale. These are terms that we rarely think of, however as you expire, you are creating space for inspiration to enter. The old stale air, thoughts, habits and behaviour can with the breath be sent to the ground, and you can fill your chakras with inspiring thoughts and ideas.

Life begins and ends with a breath. As a baby enters the world, it draws in that first breath to announce it has arrived. Its lungs fill with air, and the first part of life outside of the womb can begin. At the end of your life cycle, the breath goes, and your spirit moves on. As you take each breath, you move your life along.

Every day we breathe without even noticing, in and out. It's a part of our bodies natural rhythm and something we take for granted until we find ourselves short of breath or a feeling of tightness. Isn't it interesting how something so critical to life goes on without you even thinking about it? Over the course of the day, you will be breathing on average over 21,000 times.

Breathing is as necessary to life as your heart pumping blood through your body. These two vital organs are closely connected to the heart chakra and what we need to keep the love flowing. The Heart Chakra is associated with the element of air, which makes sense as the heart chakra also governs the lungs and breathing.

You may have thought that your breath is just your breath, but there is a difference between the energy of anyone who is breathing correctly and someone who is not. When you are breathing in a limited way, you may notice that your life feels like it is not flowing. Certainly, when it comes to journaling, I find being connected to my breath very liberating and freeing.

Breathing is not an intellectual process, we do it naturally and unconsciously. What we are looking to do, however, is to bring our conscious awareness to it and be more mindful of how we are breathing. When you slow down to journal and focus on your breath, you will feel a big difference to the way in which you journal and write.

Have you noticed when you are running around like a headless chicken and your mind is racing that your breath feels short? Sometimes you might feel like you are holding your breath, waiting for something to happen. It's as if holding your breath is holding your life together as you wait for the axe to fall. That rigidity will show up in how you live your life and how well your body functions. You will not feel nourished, your lungs will not stretch out to their full capacity, making it hard to get that vital air in.

But imagine what happens when you let it go when you slow down and savour each breath. What happens when you surrender, stop, take a deep breath, notice what is going on, and take a long slow exhale? It's quite interesting when you start to follow the breath around your body, noticing where you are holding tension and unhelpful thoughts.

Working with the breath, breathing in life will help you to stay grounded, focused and will help to reduce stress. As a result, you will sleep better, and your body will be better able to remain calm and help you to find inner peace and stability.

If you practise yoga, you may have heard of prana. Prana in Sanskrit is known as the vital life force that sustains life. In our physical body, blood flows through veins, capillaries, and arteries. The main job of red blood cells is to carry oxygen from the lungs to the body tissues and carbon dioxide as a waste product, away from the tissues and back to the lungs.

In our energy body, prana flows through energy pathways. Prana flows with the breath, so when we breathe in, we take in prana and are flowing life force around our body. You will have heard of pranayama in yoga, and this is a breathing technique which does this. Your chakras are a vital part of this process so that when your breath and prana is flowing, you will feel a greater sense of well-being.

This may be the first time you have stopped to think about your breath, take a moment to express your gratitude that your body has been doing this naturally all your life for you. Also, be thankful that it is now going to help you make more of your journaling practise.

So, let's get breathing into your heart and into your roots. Close your eyes and take your focus to your heart. It probably feels a bit odd to do it if you never have. Start by sending roots from your feet into the heart of Mother Earth, breathe up through these roots and into your heart. It may take a bit of practice, keep trying.

Notice what happens when you focus on your heart and your roots. With just a few conscious deep breaths into the heart and your roots, you will find that the heart rate decreases and your mind stops running. When you have got the hang of that, ask what messages your soul has for you. All this means is that while you concentrate on breathing into your heart, you silently ask questions. Wait and see what comes up for you. There may be something, or there may be nothing. With practice, which is what you will be doing, the messages will start coming, and you will start getting some great aha moments. That's what your journal is for, noting down what comes up, no matter how insignificant it may seem.

Journaling and breathing go together, and when you practise writing with the breath, what might have been a dull, boring and mechanical practice suddenly comes alive, as your mind expands and brings you hidden treasures.

Practising journaling using your breath as the starting point and the focus, not only opens your awareness to the present moment, which is what the breath (and inspiration) is all about, but it can also naturally put you in touch with more peace, joy, strength and your divine inner wisdom — which you may never have known you had.

Once you've become practised at breathing mindfully before writing, you will find that it becomes natural for you and of course it is available at any time. Simply combining your breathing with whatever you are doing will help you transition into a mindful state of being where you will be able to link to spirit. The practice will become a part of you and your daily life.

Journal it: As you practice your breathing exercises and meditations, be sure to record in your journal what you observe. Start by breathing into your roots and up into your heart.

Exercises to connect you with your breath

The vagus nerve

Think of the vagus nerve like a communications superhighway. It carries information between the brain and your internal organs which then controls the body's responses in times of rest and relaxation. Which is why in meditation, you will be asked to place your tongue behind your teeth to calm down your chattering mind. Try it now, it will feel weird, but notice how you calm down.

Box breathing

This is super easy and very calming. Breathe in for four, hold a full breath for four, breath out for four, hold an empty breath for four.

Prana breathing

Prana breathing or the' complete breath', uses the full capacity of the lungs.
- Place the hands on the lower abdomen, just below the navel
- Inhale breath through the nose (both nostrils) into the lower belly, the hands should move slightly out, as the diaphragm is pushing the organs in the abdominal region down and slightly out
- Now the lower abdomen is full of air, continue the breath in an upward motion to the upper chest
- Stop when the upper chest is full of breath for a second or two
- Exhale slowly from the chest out through the nose
- Stop for several seconds with empty lungs before inhaling a new breath
- Repeat this cycle as necessary. This constitutes one breathing cycle

Mindful breathing to soothe an issue

Get comfortable and close your eyes, take a gentle breath, feeling the air going in through your nostrils, into your body, and out of your nose. Connect your roots to Mother Earth and feel connected and grounded. Breathe in from your roots and into your heart.

Breathe in, say, 'Breathing in, I am calm and connected to the feelings I am experiencing now.' Breathe out, say, 'Breathing out, I am calm and connected to the feelings I am experiencing now.'

Allow yourself to feel the feelings; let them be there. Open your awareness to the breath going in, and the breath going out; only focus on this: breath in, breath out. Let the breath take its course, and don't control it in any way; just notice it.

Let your in-breath and your out-breath fill your mind. That is being mindful of your breath. Keep noticing your in-breath, your out-breath and feel the breath soothing you, comforting you and nurturing you. Feel the inner peace that this brings.

Now surrender the issue that is concerning you to this inner peace, let it flow and let the problem go. Keep breathing, noticing your in-breath and your out-breath… When you are ready, put pen to paper.

When the worry or the feeling comes back into your mind and troubles you, repeat the process, noticing and feeling your in-breath and your out-breath, while letting your breath fill your mind. Keep gently repeating this process whenever the worry or the feeling comes back until eventually, it fades away.

Spirit connection breathing exercise

Put your feet on the floor, if you can. If you have your legs up, just make sure your legs are uncrossed. Sit upright, put your shoulders back and let them relax. Notice where there is any tension, perhaps in your jaw and let go.

Imagine that roots are growing from your feet, send them into Mother Earth and feel them lock into the centre of the earth. Now breathe in from the centre of the earth up through your feet, and up to your heart. Now put your tongue on the roof of your mouth and blow out with a sigh through your mouth. As you blow out, pull your belly in. It's ok you will get used to it. Do this a few times.

Next, put one hand on your heart and one and your belly. Feel for a heart connection. The hand on your heart will centre you and the one on your belly will help you to ground. Open your mouth wide (you may hear a little crack) and breathe in. Then breathe out through your mouth with an ahh. Do this a few times, and then you are ready to write.

Choose the breathing exercises that most resonate with you. The most important thing is to connect to your breath, ground with your roots, centre at your heart and inner wisdom before you put pen to paper.

Meditation

Meditation is what you make it. The benefits are well known. You will lower your stress levels, find a place of calm and peace within, get to hear what your body (especially your heart) is saying, focus improves and best of all you are kinder to yourself.

There are so many ways to meditate. My favourite ways are to listen to a guided meditation on my Insight Timer app, to sit silently and focus on my breath with my mala beads and walking in nature. I like simple and in the moment. I do short connecting meditations before I write. Another favourite, especially for the heart, is the Metta meditation which means loving-kindness.

The way that I see meditation is that there is something for everyone, and when you find what works, you will reap the benefits. I like meditation because it needs no special equipment or set up, apart from getting into a comfortable position. Importantly I have no set outcome, more that I breathe, surrender and let it flow.

The three hearts meditation

Do this before you start your journaling practice. Find a comfortable place to sit or lie. Close your eyes. Take some deep breaths, in through the nose and out through the mouth, with a sigh and pursed lips. Become aware of your body from head to toe, of your weight, of the heaviness of your limbs. Relax. Scan your body and simply notice. Become aware of any sensations or feelings, but do not judge.

- Place your hands on your heart and breathe slowly in through the nose and out through the mouth

- I invite you to imagine that you have roots growing from your feet into Mother Earth. See them flow all the way into the centre of the Earth where you will find the heart of Mother Earth – connect with her
- Drink this energy in through your roots and into your body
- You are now securely anchored into the ground. Feel yourself becoming grounded
- Bring your attention back to your roots, allow a sense of security, calm and inner peace to come in
- Breathe in goodness and breathe out any negative things that you may be holding inside you. Send it to Mother Earth to be transmuted
- Do this for a few times
- Next, continue to breathe in healing earth energy and extend it from the base of your spine, up through your body, connecting with your heart
- Breathe in and out a few times, feel yourself becoming centred
- On your next breath, take your awareness out through the top of your head, into the heavens and the heart of consciousness and breathe in pure white light
- Flood your body with the pure white light
- Breathe out anything that does not serve you, that you may be holding inside you
- Do this for a few times
- Bring your attention back to your heart. Simply be aware. Feel, see, or sense the energy in this area. Look around, what do you notice? What messages are you getting? What images do you see? What are you sensing?
- Take a releasing breath and come back into the room

The Mala breath meditation

For this one, you need mala beads. Sit somewhere comfortable and hold your mala beads between your fingers. Move along each bead as you breathe in and out. Concentrate and breathe slowly. On the inhale extend your tummy out and on the exhale bring your tummy in. Breathe in through the nose and out through the nose or pursed lips – whichever you prefer. There are 108 beads on your necklace, and in the time you take to move through all of them, you will find a place of inner peace.

Balancing chakra meditation

Find a comfortable place to sit or lie. Close your eyes. Take some deep breaths, in through the nose and out through the mouth, with a sigh. Become aware of your body from head to toe, of your weight, of the heaviness of your limbs. Relax. Scan your body and simply notice. Become aware of any sensations or feelings, but do not judge.

I invite you to imagine that you have roots growing from your feet into the heart of Mother Earth. See them flow all the way into the centre of the Earth where there is a pot of grounding and healing energy. Drink this energy in through your roots and into your body. You are now securely anchored into the ground. Feel yourself becoming grounded. Bring your attention back to your root chakra, allow a sense of security, calm and inner peace to come in.

Imagine a shaft of light extending from the base of your spine and travelling into the centre of the earth, to your core essence and the pot of grounding and healing energy. Breathe in goodness and breathe out any negative things that you may be holding inside you. Send it to Mother Earth to be transmuted. Do this for a few times.

Next, continue to breathe in healing earth energy and extend it from the base of your spine, up through your body and into each of your chakras, balancing each as you go and out through the top of your head, into the heavens and the heart of consciousness and breathe in pure white light. Flood your body with the pure white light. Breathe out anything that does not serve you, that you may be holding inside you. Do this for a few times.

Bring your attention back to your heart chakra. Simply be aware. Feel, see, or sense the energy in this area. Look around, what do you notice?

- What messages are you getting?
- What images do you see?
- What are you feeling?
- What are you sensing?
- What do you just know?
- What do you feel gratitude and appreciation for?

Take as long as you like, and when you feel grounded, centred and balanced, you can start to write in your journal. When you have finished writing, breathe love into your heart chakra, around your body and chakras, back to your heart and out through your heart into the world. As you go about your day, remember that you are surrounded by love and can breathe that in and out into the world whenever you need to.

As you become comfortable with connecting with your chakras, start to feel into your chakras in a more curious way. By that I mean, perhaps take a bit more time to notice, or have a few more conversations with them, play with the energy and have fun.

Metta meditation

The Dhammapada, which is a collection of Buddha's sayings, says, "Hatred cannot coexist with love and kindness. It dissipates when supplanted with thoughts of love and compassion."

The loving-kindness or Metta meditation is a powerful and seemingly simple meditation that enables us to foster love, affection, appreciation and kindness towards ourselves, others and the world. With this meditation, there are no expectations, it is a process to enjoy, where you let go, let love and let flow. We start with ourselves because if we cannot love ourselves, how can we love others. I am sure that you will find it healing and calming.

The way that I use it is to focus on me first so that I reach a place of love and appreciation for me as I go about my day.

When I first started this practice, I was surprised that the husband I left after discovering his double life was easy to pass loving kindness on to. However, the long term partner before was difficult and brought some feelings of anger. I stuck at it and slowly and believe me it was slow, I eventually let go.

When it came to people that I had a difficult time with I chose to reframe. I didn't need them in my life and go to lunch with them, but I could choose to see them through the lens of love and know that harbouring unkind feelings towards them was hurting me more.

Sending love to the world is far more manageable. Although I did feel helpless because I couldn't stop all of the cruelty that I was witness to. What I could do was to send my love out and release it to a higher power who would know where to send it.

Read through the meditation and practice in a way that works for you, always starting with and including you.

Get ready to Metta

Find a comfortable place to sit or lie. Close your eyes. Take some deep breaths, in through the nose and out through the mouth, with a sigh. Become aware of your body from head to toe, of your weight, and of the heaviness of your limbs. Relax. Scan your body and simply notice. Become aware of any sensations or feelings, but do not judge.

I invite you to imagine that you have roots growing from your feet into the heart of Mother Earth. See them flow all the way into the centre of the Earth where there is a pot of grounding and healing energy. Drink this energy in through your roots and into your body. You are now securely anchored into the ground. Feel yourself becoming grounded. Breathe up and into your heart. Breathe out. Do a few rounds of this.

Directed to yourself

You begin with yourself because without loving yourself, it is difficult to love others.

    May I be filled with loving-kindness

    May I be held in loving kindness

    May I accept myself as I am

    May I be happy

    May I know the joy of being alive

    Repeat this as many times as you feel you need and then move on to the next step.

Directed to someone you like/ love

When you feel you have established some stronger sense of loving-kindness for yourself, you can then expand your meditation to include others. After focusing on yourself for five or ten minutes, choose a benefactor, someone in your life who has loved and genuinely cared for you. Picture this person and carefully recite the same phrases:

    May you be filled with loving-kindness

    May you be held in loving kindness

May you accept yourself as you are

May you be happy

May you know the joy of being alive

Repeat this as many times as you feel you need and then move on to the next step.

After this, you can include others: Spend some time wishing well to a wider circle of friends.

Directed to the world and globally

Then gradually extend your meditation to picture and include community members, neighbours, people everywhere, animals, all beings, the whole earth.

May we be filled with loving-kindness

May we be held in loving kindness

May we accept ourselves as we are

May we be happy

May we know the joy of being alive

Repeat this as many times as you feel you need and then move on to the next step.

Directed to someone who challenges you

Finally, include the difficult people in your life, even your enemies, wishing that they too may be filled with loving-kindness and peace. This will take practice. But as your heart opens, first to loved ones and friends, you will find that in the end, you won't want to close it anymore.

May you be filled with loving-kindness

May you be held in loving kindness

May you accept yourself as you are

May you be happy

May you know the joy of being alive

Repeat this as many times as you feel you need.

That's it, one of the most powerful meditations I know and one which will I am sure will change your life as well.

Journaling prompts

- Sit quietly for a few minutes, just breathing and listening to your body. What is it telling you? Where do you feel strong, healthy, energetic, relaxed? Where do you feel tense, worried, uncomfortable, tired? What is asking for more attention?
- Which parts of your life do you need to breathe more life into?
- Which chakras need more breath in them?
- What happens when you breathe into each chakra?
- What are the magical moments that take your breath away, and how can you capture more of these?
- Spell BREATHE and make each letter form a random word. Then freewrite for 10 minutes including these words

Journaling magic

With the right words and the right intentions, it's easy to create something magical

What better way to start your journaling practise than to greet your journal. We do these prompts to bring super positive energy to your journal. I believe that journals are living things and need to be set up to receive whatever is coming over its life. This is foundational journaling magic. As you start to do more writing and reflecting in your journal, you need to consider how to bring magic to your daily practice. Get yourself a brand new journal. Pick one that you would love to write in. I don't believe in using cheap notebooks, because you want your journaling practice to reflect the value that you place on yourself.

Rituals for new journals

I usually start a new journal at the beginning of the month, sometimes at a new moon or at the start of a new journaling project. This book is what I'd call a journaling project. The ritual goes like this:

- Bring energy and intentions to your journal
- Expectations and feelings
- Create or revise your bucket list for your soul
- Design or revise your life focus areas

- Where am I?
- Who do you want to be?
- What do you want to create?
- What does my future self know?
- Discover or reconnect to your big life goal, dream or desire
- What other goals do you have?
- Creating or reconnecting with your vision
- Checking in with your values
- What is the next aligned step?
- Successes and celebrations

Bring energy and intentions to your journal

All of my journals are living breathing beings that hold my vibration and essence. Before I use a journal, I want to bless it and create intentions for it. The simplest way to do this is to hold it in your hands and breathe love into it. Go to the first page of your journal and write your intentions. I also colour in a hand mandala and write my intentions and affirmations around it.

Expectations and feelings

What are the start of your journal expectations? How are you feeling? What thoughts do you have as you enter this phase? What would make it go well? What outcomes do you want? How do you want to feel when you reach the end of the month?

Journal it: As you start your journal, what are your expectations let the energy of your desires flow to the Universe?

Brainstorming your bucket list for the soul

At the start of each new journal (month, new moon), it's a great idea to think about what you want. The things on your list can be anything, the point is for you to just scribble and to keep scribbling. These can be anything from new shoes, the windows painted, to a baby, a new job or change in business direction, better health, self-love, inner peace, or meeting your soul mate. Just get them all out. Why anything? Because often, what we desire has a deeper fundamental meaning. New shoes could be about self-esteem, new doors – safety, or a holiday – you need to unwind and escape from the day to day stress. Start with the mundane, move on the material and finish with the magical. Keep coming back and adding things in. This is great fun, and you will end up with all kinds of things on your list. If you are stuck for inspiration, take a look at the life focus areas in the next section.

Journal it: Write your bucket list – start with the mundane, move to material and end with the magical.

Life focus areas

Life focus areas are where we want to create areas of attention. Look at your bucket list, which of these items fit into these life focus areas? These are a suggestion to kickstart you. Take a look, do any resonate or do you have different life focus areas that are important to you?

- Health and wellbeing
- Learning
- Financial
- Heart and spirit

- Experiences
- Mental/emotional
- Love/Partner
- Family
- Friends
- Mission/Vision

Your focus for the journey ahead

Once you have reviewed your bucket list, you will probably find that you have a different set of life focus areas that are important to you that you want to focus on. Go through your list and write down the life focus areas that you want to focus on. You can come back and refine them later on. Take your time. You may find that these will change. These are mine:

- Health and wellbeing
- Love and marriage
- Business (structure, strategy and success)
- Novels and writing
- Wealth (health, financial, social, spiritual)
- Spirituality (me and my space)
- Inspiration – being of service
- Relationship with me and others
- Community
- Creativity

When you get to daily journaling, you will start to use these as the focus for your daily aligned actions (to do's) for the day ahead. Don't freak you don't need actions in everyone – just the priority ones for the day. Either print your focus areas out and glue them into the front of your journal or write them out as a reminder. I write each one in a different colour.

Journal it: Think about the things you want, look at your bucket list for inspiration. When you have done that, create the list of life focus areas you want to place your attention on.

Put your list into life focus areas

When I have my life focus areas, I go back through my bucket list with a coloured pen and mark them up. Anything that doesn't fit is probably mundane or material. All of these categories are important. For example, there are lots of things around the house that need doing, I put these on my material list, put them in order of priority, set a budget and time frame and tick them off, one by one. You will find that as you do this, certain ones will jump out as priorities.

Journal it: Go back to your bucket list and mark them up with your life focus area categories. Anything that doesn't fit could be the mundane or the material – simply mark these like that.

Where am I?

Put a stake in the ground and look around. This may seem very simple, but it is, in fact, very powerful and may bring up all kinds of feelings. You must look around you and take it all in. Simply acknowledge that this is where you find yourself. Describe where you find yourself. Consider how this feels. What do you see and what do you know about this place? I do this when I am feeling a bit lost, as well.

Take a look at these life focus areas and mark yourself 0 (it's a bit rubbish) to 10 (yahoo all is well in my world). If you have created your own list, write these out and do a check against them.

- Health and wellbeing
- Learning
- Financial
- Heart and spirit
- Experiences
- Mental/emotional
- Love/Partner
- Family
- Friends
- Mission/Vision

When you consider each of the areas, ask how much energy, time, or the effort you are putting in. What works for me is energy, what might work for you is time and effort. For example, a high number in the finances does not necessarily mean that I'm well off but instead means that I take good care of this area, spend responsibly, etc. The key is to make these your own so that when you undertake a review, you can say mmm last month I was doing great on managing my finances, why aren't I now? You may see that another area has also been neglected, e.g. your health, and this is what has impacted your finances. You will then see that in this case, you must address your health to bring the finances back into balance, and this is your priority

Journal it: Describe where you are. Consider how this feels. What do you see and what do you know about this place? Mark your life focus areas out of ten.

Who do you want to be?

This may look and feel like a difficult question, but it isn't really. It is iterative because every time you go through personal transformation, you find out a bit more about you. For years I wanted to be someone who inspired others to write books. Then I discovered that what I really wanted was to be someone who wanted to inspire others to embrace the magic of who they are so that they could find out what they wanted and who they wanted to be, and I want to be a novelist.

Looking at who you are now, be really truthful and speak from your heart. It could be a supportive and loving partner, a shining light to your children and someone who inspires them to follow their dreams. You may want to be a leader of some sort – what kind? You might just want to be kinder and more compassionate and perhaps a little less judgemental. You can use the life focus areas to help you.

Journal it: This is a beautiful question – who do you want to be? You already know the answer. Let it flow.

What do you want to create?

Creation is about envisioning. Shortly you will be writing about your perfect day. But first, kick start the process by asking the question, what do I want to create? Often if you can't see it, you can't create it. Think about how it will make you feel when you have what you want. The Universe will respond to the energy of what you put out. This is a question I ask all of my clients when we start working together because it gives me an idea of what is in their hearts, and it starts them wondering what is possible for them. I want to create a community of conscious people who use writing and energy work to discover what they want, who they want to be, heal, find meaning and purpose and go on to inspire others to know what is possible in the world.

Journal it: What do you want to create? How will you feel when you have created it and who will you be?

What my future self knows

Your future you is very wise. Ask a question. There are two ways that you can do this:

- Use the three hearts meditation to go into a meditative state and join your future self for a chat. What does he/she tell you that you need to know? Look around the place that you meet in and get a good idea of where they live, what the place they meet you in is like – colours – furniture – décor, etc. What do they look like?
- Write a question in your journal, dear future self can you tell me…? Then sleep on it. Literally, put your journal under your pillow. When you wake in the morning, write the answer

Journal it: Go to a future version of you and ask them any burning questions you have, knowing that you already know the answer. There is no such thing as a wrong decision or wrong answer. When you consider your questions, ask if are you choosing from love or fear? Then ask what the next right step is? Ask clarifying questions. Make sure you are connected with the energy of it already being done and then making decisions from that version of you. What do you need to get you to where you need to be?

What is your big life goal, dream or desire

When you look at your bucket list and life focus areas, what is the one thing that stands out and screams – me, me, me? This will be the 'thing' that I call your big life goal, dream or desire. This is a great moment to step back and consider if the things you are doing and the things in your life are serving you. Start by reviewing your bucket list and then asking your heart what your big life goal, dream or desire is. See it as done and then say, and so it is done. Your big life goal, dream or desire will often come from the magical part of your bucket list. Look at your list and intuitively pick that one big thing. For example, when I look at my bucket list, I know that writing novels is my BIG dream. This is my prime focus outside of my business and life goals. To enable me to achieve this, I need to create conditions that allow me to do it. Underneath this big life dream sits smaller goals and other desires.

The key thing to remember is that a dream written down with a date becomes a goal. A goal with daily aligned actions helps you to make your dreams come true. To make this work, your big dream or desire needs to become a goal.

Journal it: Write out your big life goal, dream or desire, get out your coloured pens and make it bigger and brighter. What do you see, feel, sense or know? Who will you be when you are living this goal, dream or desire? Explore.

What other goals do you have?

As well as your big life goal, dream or desire, there may be other goals that come from your bucket list. The key with goals is to not have too many, or you will become overwhelmed, and then nothing will get done. I like to have a focus for the next 90 days. Goals are a roadmap to a place you want to go, they are future-focused and something you want to create in the world.

Journal it: Choose two other goals to focus on for the next 90 days.

Creating future magic

You could set goals using the SMART system, but we are going to create our goals by creating future magic. Magic stands for:

- M – Measurable
- A – Aligned action
- G – Grounded in reality
- I – Inspired and inspiring. Is this goal, dream or desire consistent with your values?
- C – Clarity

An example for writing a novel might be:

- M – written by March 20xx
- A – create a plan, outline, write, edit and publish, with dates beside each action

- G –given everything else I need to do, the deadline is achievable
- I – becoming a novelist inspires me – it is my big life dream, and it will inspire others
- C – I am clear on the specifics, which are – I have written a book called xxx, by xxx, I have my action plan, steps and I know what it will give me, how I will feel and who I will become

Journal it: Apply the magic formula to your goals and then check in with your heart that these feel congruent with who you are and what you want. Is this goal, dream or desire in alignment with your truth, heart and soul? How does it contribute to your health, wellbeing, happiness and long term vision for your life?

Envisioning what you want

Connect to your heart, bring in what you want to create, who you want to be, your big life goal, dream or desire, life focus areas and bucket list and then write about your perfect day. This is an imaginary day, sometime in the future, where you have everything you want. You've achieved every desire you could ever have; you live exactly where you want, and with the person or people, you want to be with and have everything you want. Write it as if it were already true and here. Remember to date it and say thank you. Have fun.

Your unconscious mind doesn't know the difference between reality and imagination if they are both fuelled by an emotional response, so it's important to fully engage with the sights, smells, tastes, sounds and the feel of the situation you are imagining because reality involves all the senses.

And, once you set out a clear description of your perfect day, and focus on it often, your unconscious mind will do everything it can to balance out the reality it sees with the reality it has been shown. Once you have the story of your perfect day set in stone by bringing it to mind often. You will soon be able to recall the story at will.

Bringing it alive

- Create a scene in your mind of an imaginary movie theatre. Imagine yourself sitting in the centre of the front row
- In front of you is a large screen and on it is the start of your perfect day story

- Start the movie and run your story all the way to the end
- At the end of the movie, freeze the last frame
- Turn up the colours, the brightness and the sounds and imagine yourself walking into the movie on the screen
- Fully absorb yourself into the "you" on the screen
- Restart the movie and enter your perfect day
- Run the movie through several times at normal speed while experiencing all of the wonderful colours, sounds and experiences of the new you. See the sights, hear the sounds and feel the feelings
- Then freeze the last frame
- Repeat the process until this feels like the real you

This technique lets your unconscious mind know that this is your reality and will now make everything in the movie happen. Read through your perfect day often and rerun the visualisation exercise several times. Muse on this as you go about your day. You can even do this as part of your daily meditation or walk. And don't forget to watch for the changes that show up in your life, and record these in your journal.

Finally, plant your perfect day in a small plant pot or perhaps a candle holder, add in things that feel enriching. I, for example, would add crystals, you could add in hearts and light a candle. If you have an altar put your pot on there.

Journal it: Write about your about perfect day and bring it alive. When you have done that plant it.

Successes and celebrations

Head to the back of your journal and write – success and celebrations. Remember to go their as soon as you have a success or feel that you want to record a celebration.

Let the magic of believing in yourself guide your life

Daily magic

Every day I feel the magic of life surround me

Getting into a good routine for the day will make all the difference to your day and to your life. When you are journaling, consider:-

- Your goals, dreams and desires
- Where you are and what you want to create in your life
- Who you want to be
- How you want to feel about your life
- What you are open to giving and receiving
- How gratitude, appreciation and your blessings are helping you to learn more about you and the way you live your life
- What daily aligned actions you will take?
- What you want to let go of
- Time for reflection

How to design daily magic

Journal as often as you can, but don't put yourself under pressure, and if you miss a day – start again the next day. I love starting my day with an affirmation, envisioning what I want and ending it with reflection and my gratitude practice. When I am not doing my gratitude practice, I will either freewrite, pick a prompt or choose an oracle card. I make journaling easy by intuitively following what needs to come to the paper. And if I do not want to journal for a day, I don't. On these days, I may connect to my future self or my guides, ask a question and go to sleep, knowing that in the morning, I will have some answers.

The most important thing about creating a daily routine is designing one that works for you. There is loads of advice about how to make this work, but unless you understand how you tick, none of them is going to work.

Freewrite or structure?

Freewrite

Freewriting is a way to let whatever needs to meet the page flow. The key is to relax, breathe, ground and centre first and then write. I have a method for getting to the heart of what needs to come out, and that is to start writing about the mundane and allowing the magic to flow. The idea is that you let your thoughts, feelings and emotions to arise without judgement and without censoring your language or words, express yourself freely. When you let go of judgement and expectations, your writing will flow, and you will feel great for having got it all out.

You can use freewriting to either let it all out and let the day or thing that is bugging you go, or you can choose a topic and focus on that. For example, one of my favourite freewriting exercises is to write to my heart and then ask my heart to write back to me.

Journal it: Set a timer for 10 minutes, either write to your heart or simply put pen to paper and write. Simply enjoy the process

Structure

Having a structure such as using the ideas in journaling magic to kick start your journal or month gives you a framework to write within. Using journaling prompts helps you to focus your flow, although who knows where a prompt will take you, and that's one of the things that I love about prompts is that they take you into the realms of freewriting.

Journal it: Set a timer for 10 minutes, put pen to paper and answer this question – what was the best thing about today?

Mornings

For some people, mornings are often a mad rush to get out of the door and into work. They don't need to be like that if perhaps you planned a bit more. Of course, that is easy to say, you might have a million and one things tugging at your energy and time. However, you need to figure out what needs to be done and then when and how you are going to do it.

Evenings

One of the reasons that I journal at night is that in the morning I like to do my grounding and centring work, perhaps a mental visit to my future self or visualising my day, and then I have two dogs to take for a walk. They will harass me until I obey them. Also journaling at night allows me to let go of the day. Here are things that I do:

- Three times a week (every other day-ish), I look at my focus areas and intuitively choose a few areas that I need to do something with and write one thing I need to do to ensure I am taking aligned action. Remember, these focus areas came from my bucket list
- Three times a week, I write what I am grateful for (up to 3)
- Pull an oracle card and write about what that means to me
- Pick a prompt
- Ask a question for my future self or guides
- Freewrite

The key for me is to do what feels good in the moment. In this way, journaling remains a joy. The way I look at it is that no matter how disciplined you are, life can get in the way. I like to think more about how I use my energy rather what time I have to do things by. To make this work for me, I use my most productive times (the morning) for my most challenging tasks. This means that once I have walked the dogs, I feel energised to get to work. By the afternoon, my energy is dipping.

Think about it, we all have a finite amount of energy available to us. Energy management is just as important as how you manage your time. What is also important is making sure that you get good quality sleep so that you can follow any routines that you set up for yourself.

Having no routine or structure can be mentally draining as you will continuously be catching up, procrastinating, missing essential things and possibly letting others down. Designing a daily routine that works for you is an investment in your personal growth, inner peace and contentment and a way to be your best self.

Habits like journaling can support how you live your life, manage your energy and help you to achieve what you desire. Never be afraid to experiment with your habits and see how they will work for you. If they support you to feel energised then great and if they don't try another way. New research suggests that you need to do something for 66 days to create a habit.

Becoming a regular journaler requires focus and discipline. This can seem like someone is bossing you around, and you may feel resistance. Examine where that resistance is coming from – yes even journal on it. Then do something about it. The biggest takeaway from this is – design your routine, experiment with it and make it work for you. And start a new journal with the right vibration. Once you have done this, you will be ready to practice affirmations, gratitude, daily prompts and free writing.

Journal it: Explore what a great routine would look like to you and remember to add in why it will work.

Your daily affirmation – roots and foundations

When you do add in an affirmation (see later), stay focused on it during your day. Here is a selection from the affirmations chapter. Choose one of these or make up your own. I feel deeply rooted

- I feel safe and secure
- I belong
- I have what I need
- I am attracting an abundance of money
- I am financially free
- I am connected with nature
- I allow myself to be nourished and supported by Mother Earth
- I trust that my needs will always be met

Journal it: Create an affirmation that holds meaning for you. You could also turn your affirmation into a question and explore. E.g. I trust myself to do the right thing. How can I trust myself to do the right thing?

Envisioning your day

When you have your affirmation ask - how you would like your day to be, and what do you want? I find visualising about how I would like my day to be as if all of the wonderful things have already happened extremely powerful. If you have chosen to write about how you will visualise your day, carry on describing and feeling what you have so that you bring it alive. Choose words that are vivid and light you up. Think about how you feel and pull that into your heart space.

Journaling prompts

There are lots of journaling prompts later in the book. Pick a prompt for the day and write for five to ten minutes. Always be guided and pick a prompt that resonates, rather than forcing it.

What is the next aligned action for your life focus areas?

When you look at your life focus areas, ask what is my next aligned action for the ones you want to focus on. What I do is scan my life focus areas which I have written on the inside cover of my journal and ask which one or ones do I need to focus on and what is the ONE thing I need to do today. Check-in with any blocks and resistance you have to getting things done and ask why – this is a wonderful way to check in to see if these things are really what you want to be focusing on or if you need to do some digging. When you assess your aligned actions, what do you notice as you go from day to day, week to week or month to month? E.g.

- *Health and wellbeing – start juicing with celery* *
- Love and marriage
- Business (structure, strategy and success)
- *Novels and writing – do a character sketch* *
- *Wealth (health, financial, social, spiritual) – start a money tracker* *
- Spirituality (me and my space)

- Inspiration – being of service
- Relationship with me and others
- Community
- Creativity

Journal it: Describe your next aligned actions where relevant. Always remember to say thank you for what you already have. AND remember to do them… If your aligned actions, don't get done – explore why.

End of the week reflections

At the end of the week, reflect on some of the things you have written about and how they have impacted your life. What have you learned about you? What are your most significant insights?

Before you start to write, read through your week and simply become aware of anything that stands out for you, focus on your affirmations, prompts and colours you choose to colour in the mandala with, and ask what do you learn from these things? When you have mused, you are ready to reflect on your week.

86

Journaling ideas and prompts

I have what I need to inspire me

Here are a few more journaling ideas to whet your appetite.

Questions – about your day

Aside from the other prompts, you could try these about my day questions. Things are so much easier if someone asks us questions. Try these now to get a feel for responding to questions. What do you learn about you in this process?

- How did the day begin?
- What happened as the day progressed?
- What is today's story?
- What is the best thing that happened?
- What am I grateful for today?
- How did the day end?

The about your day questions will help you to start to recognise patterns and pictures about you and your life. You may find yourself stuck in a story that seems endless, and this is when reflecting back over your week can highlight any sticky stuckness.

Looking for inspiration

Words for the month, week or day

Sometimes when you are stumped for something to journal about, even if you have a prompt, it can be easier to pick a word each day, journal about what it means to you and then look at what comes up for you during the day.

Balance, abundance, beauty, love, courage, confidence, strength, enlightenment, focus, energy, succulent, colourful, lush, positivity, joy, motivation, determination, stability, reason, self-care, breathless, nurturing, sultry, simplicity, kindness, zest, affection, empathy, rapport, soft, sweet, gentle, earthy, modest. Reflect on your word at the end of the day.

Doodling

When you can't find the words, doodle. Doodling essentially allows our intuitive feelings to come out in pictures and symbols. Interpreting these pictures and symbols can help to reveal meanings that are not apparent to our linear mind. A picture or symbol conveys an entire thought in one image. While doodling, words may form themselves, and these should be accepted. But, for the most part, doodling allows the unconscious to come to the surface without judgment or critical analysis from the conscious mind. Therefore, if you find yourself doodling, that's great, carry on.

Mind Mapping

When I want to explore an idea, thought or feeling, I simply create a mind map. A mind map is a collection of thoughts around a central idea. It is quick and simple and serves to ignite my imagination. I also use it for creating plans and developing ideas.

5-word mind-map

This is very simple and is similar to the mind mapping idea, except the word is a word for today. You write a word in the middle of the page and then allow five other words to come and on each branch five and five more until you run out. Then you can write about what comes up for you.

Spelling out words

Spelling out words is also a brilliant way of getting your brain engaged. You could use the word of the day or pick a word that you want to explore. E.g.

- L - Life
- O - Open
- V - Values
- E – Evolve

Journal it: Pick one of these journaling ideas and have a go.

Deepen your practice

Once you have written something, go back and highlight things of interest and curiosity. When you have done that, pick one thing and write for 10 minutes.

Do not dwell in the past, do not dream of the future, concentrate the mind on the present moment. Buddha

Mandalas

My life is colourful and magical

The word mandala comes from the ancient Sanskrit language, and it means "circle" or "centre". They have been used for centuries in rituals and for meditation. While they look like interesting shapes, there is much more to a mandala than that. If you look around at nature, you will see that there are all kinds of unusual shapes. Bring a snowflake to mind or a spider's web. These are both intricate and beautiful, and when you look at them, you may find yourself transported into a world of wonder.

Colouring mandalas (or other mandala type images) has been proven to produce a calming effect on the person colouring them in. Journaling and reflective writing have also been shown to have a profound effect on the writer. Putting the two together is incredibly healing. The very act of colouring releases tension and allows your unconscious thoughts to flow. When you then write about what comes up, you will get incredible insights. Then upon reflection, you begin to make sense, see patterns, ways through your problems and onto to solutions, ideas and inspiration.

Combining colouring mandalas with journaling and reflective writing will change your perspective and your life. Then, if you choose, you can make some significant changes based on what you learn.

You will discover mandalas (or other mandala type images) throughout the book alongside an affirmation. These are your pause for thought moments. Coming back to the present and being mindful gives your busy mind a chance to go ahhhh.

Why colour mandalas?

What I love about mandalas is the sense of wellbeing that I get when I focus on them and colour them in. I will typically tune into something that is on my mind, connect to my muse, set an intention and then allow whatever needs to flow, arise.

Mandalas offer you the opportunity to focus in on something and then work your way out from the centre to the outer edges where your consciousness is expanded. Imagine that the centre is the issue and as you work out, you are discovering solutions.

When you concentrate on an aspect of your life, you are energetically connecting to your inner state, intuition, wisdom and creativity, which is then reflected back in not only the process that you use to colour in your mandala but the colours that you use.

When you start to colour in your mandala, you will notice yourself relaxing and yourself opening up to your inner wisdom and creativity where you will find the solutions you need.

The magic of colour

All colours have an energetic vibration and meaning. Each colour radiates a certain spiritual frequency; therefore, it attracts different kinds of energy. What you will notice is that you may crave a particular colour. When I get up each morning, I know that I need to wear a specific colour. These colours are being called for because of the energy they emit. When you colour a mandala, the same thing happens.

You may have days where you reach for all of the blues and turquoises and other days when you might choose red with orange and vibrant pink. What about the language of colour. Consider red, something might be red hot, or you could be seeing red when provoked. How about mellow yellow? Feeling blue? Who is to say what this means other than you.

Rather than getting hung up on what that colour means, I believe is primarily up to you and how it makes you feel and what it means to you. If for example, when you see yellow, you think of the warming sun that makes you feel happy, then that is what it means to you. If on the other hand you see yellow and think yuk, I'd never wear it as it washes me out, then you may be unlikely to reach for the yellows in your crayon tin when colouring. I chose yellow as my example because certain yellows turn warm mustardy, autumnal yellows that I would prefer instead.

The benefits of mandalas

- There is no right or wrong way to colour a mandala. Colour them in any way you desire
- You can colour in a mandala just about anywhere there is a surface for you to rest on
- Colouring lifts your spirits and brings out the child in you
- You can colour at your own pace
- You are creating a unique work of art
- It connects you to your wisdom and creativity
- It's relaxing and will help you to destress

Try the one-minute mandala

The one-minute mandala is quite simple. Get everything ready, set a timer for one minute and colour. You won't get much done, but it's a lovely way of being aware of being mindful for a minute. Choose one of the gorgeous mandalas in this book. Each one has an affirmation with it for you to focus on. You can also download a separate pack of mandalas at https://daledarley.com/love-to-journal-roots. Choose your mandala and spend a few minutes every day being mindful. When you colour, bring to mind how you would like your day to be. This can be today or tomorrow if it's now the evening. What about that magic you want to manifest? Even if there is nothing on your mind or nothing in particular you want, choose an affirmation, start colouring it in and enjoy the process.

Reflect on your mandalas

When you look at each mandala, what are your first impressions? Go deeper, what else? What do you learn? What do you see, sense or know?

Journal it: Choose a mandala and colour it in intuitively. How did it go? What insights did you get?

When you catch a rainbow, you can fill yourself with the vibrant colour of life

Affirmations

Affirmations are the truths of our hearts and souls

I like to start my client's journaling practice with affirmations. This is a simple yet incredibly effective way to change state and create a flow towards positivity and seeing things from another perspective.

The mind is a powerful thing, and what we tell it becomes our truth. Imagine that we can tell ourselves stuff, and it becomes real. The main problem is as you already know is that we often tell ourselves rubbish things. Things like I have fat knees, my arms are ugly, who would love someone like me, people are judging me, I am unlovable and many, many more. I know how harmful these things are because I hated my body for years. I thought I was fat and ugly and my arms they were horrendous. None of it was true, but I believed it.

After many years of living like this, I was woken up, and I embarked on a massive self-love journey which supported me when my spine fractured, and I needed to heal myself. I used daily affirmations in a range of ways. One year later, I created 101 days of being me (you can sign up here https://daledarley.com/101-days-of-being-me/) which used daily affirmations to help me and now countless others to get better connected to who they are and to enjoy being their beautiful, wonderful selves.

What are affirmations?

Affirmations are things that you affirm to be true, in other words, positive statements. These statements describe something positive that you want to achieve. They are usually short sentences and are something that you can easily repeat during the day. What they do is to tell your unconscious mind that something is real. Your unconscious mind will see these positive statements, and it will be triggered into action. Try this – I have a beautiful smile. With any luck, you immediately smiled and forgot that perhaps you didn't like your teeth, for example. It's that simple and so infectious.

When you repeat affirmations, your mind finds these motivating and inspiring and trots off to obey you. Like the excellent computer that it is, it will embed these programs into its every day 'you' code, and it becomes true.

Affirmations are lovely for designing and building new habits, changing thoughts and beliefs and for healing the body. Two of my big affirmations or mantras as they are also called when I was healing my spine was, I have strong, healthy bones, and my bones are healed. I would write these on my fridge with magnetic letters.

Surprisingly people use affirmations every day without realising it. Usually, these are the not so useful ones. You may have heard others talk about limiting beliefs? That's what these are. You tell yourself that you are can't do or be something often enough your mind says oke doke, I'll add that to the program, and it will be true, and before you know it you can't do those things, or you procrastinate. Call something to mind right now that you know you always say you can't do, what if you said I can? Feels weird, right? It does take practice. One of my favourite journaling exercises is to turn I can't into I can. It is very revealing.

What we know about negative thinking is that it reinforces an internal belief that we can't change. This means that we are almost destined to continue to repeat what might be potentially self-destructive behaviours. This leads to a vicious circle of more yukky unhelpful thinking. Take a moment to imagine (see, sense, feel or know) how your life might be if you turned these around and used affirmations to reinforce the more positive aspects of who you are.

It's all about choice. You can choose to change your thinking or not. Ok, I know that years of negative programming can mean that you have a bit more work to do. But here's the secret sauce, while you may struggle to start off with, guess what, it won't take long before you are smiling to yourself as you catch those words daring to come out. Soon you will find yourself looking in the mirror and saying yes, I know I did it again, here's what I meant to say. At least this is what I do. I find staring at myself in the eyes and confessing rather amusing, and it really gives me the kick that I need.

When I worked in an office and found myself in a situation that meant I was repeating negative stuff, I'd head off the bathroom and look myself in the eye and say something positive. I'd also pull faces, as long as no one else was around. The face pulling was to make me laugh and then I could say an affirmation, anchor it in and go back to face the day.

Journal it: Ask yourself right now what would it be like if I told myself positive affirmations more often? How would it be if I did this daily? What is the first affirmation that I would choose? Write it out and say it. How does that feel?

Journaling and affirmations

Start your day with an affirmation in your journal. Write it and leave it. Later that day come back and reflect on what happened during the day as you repeated the affirmation. One of the things that I do is turn the affirmation around and ask it as a question. E.g. if the affirmation is today I am grounded, I would write how can I be more grounded today? The reason I try to add in today I am is that affirmations need to be in the now, rather than some woolly future, I will statement. Now you may have noticed that I said I try, which is also another one of those words that mean you might or you might not. An affirmation like I will try and drink more water is pretty rubbish, it would be far better to state today I am drinking water to hydrate my body and to have a juicy life.

Journal it: Write an affirmation that is in the now and turn it into a question.

Affirmations for everyday life

Now that you know that your mind likes to accept what you say and if you keep saying it these things get added to the program, there's something else you might want to know. When you repeat things, you attract things. Positive affirmations attract positive results. Before you rush and repeat, I have a beachside house, £10 million in the bank and drive a Ferrari, let me stop you. What I am talking about is affirming things that your heart and soul know to be true about you as a person, not your possessions.

Naturally, you may struggle with creating positive affirmations about yourself when you feel lousy about your self-esteem and life. I know when I looked in the mirror with a misshapen body from the fractures, it was pretty hard, in fact, impossible to say that I was gorgeous. Instead, I said things like today, I am thanking my body for knowing how to heal. Eventually, I was able to say different words. Please shape your words so that affirmations work for you in your daily life. One of my favourite affirmations is I am healthy, wealthy, healed and happy.

Journal it: Try this now, write a personal affirmation that you feel comfortable with. Then, rewrite stretching just a tiny bit out of your comfort zone. How does that feel? What do you notice?

What do you want?

If you spend your life saying I can't or words to that effect then you know that they will come true, like a self-fulfilling prophecy. What happens is that you lose sight of your goals, desires and dreams. You are more likely to move into fear, and your motivation will disappear. When you are not inspired, life can become dull and boring. You are an inspiring person; you just might not believe it just yet. Say it now, I am an inspirational person. It took me years to accept that people found me inspiring. I thought it was just my mum being kind to me.

Journal it: Let me ask you these questions:

- What do you want?
- Where do you want to go?
- What do you want to create for your life?
- How will it feel when you have what you want?
- Who will you be when you get what you want?

Big questions, aren't they? If you focus on them and ask them regularly, the answers will become more evident, and you will gain more clarity of your desires for this life. Now write an affirmation, confirming what you want.

Chatting with your most important person

You are the most important person in your life. In this life, you are here to learn some lessons and find your gifts. Life can be challenging, but in every challenge, you overcome, you can add another piece of gold to your treasure chest. You will learn more about you and how amazing you are. Now is the time to let affirmations into your life and tell yourself stuff that is true. It is vital that you say simple but powerful things so that you become them. Doing this will help you to form great habits.

In your head right now, you will be having a conversation. I'm not in your head, but I can guess some of the things that you are saying. My invitation is that you learn to observe through journaling the not so great conversations, tell them to move over and begin a more positive conversation instead. Turn your mind chatter into affirming positive thoughts and see what happens.

When my ug moments come, because let's face it life is not sitting on clouds and being fed nectar of the heavens, I chat to myself. What I do is to look at things from many angles after I have had a paddy and sworn a lot. I look for facts and ask myself how I can reframe what is going on.

In my journal, when I write these things, I consider the kind of language, words and stories that I use and what these are telling me. When you start to notice yours, you can choose to make changes. After a while, you will see them as soon as they come up in everyday life. When your new language comes up as part of your usual daily chatter, you will soon start smiling and say here I go again and, in that moment, you will be able to choose to say better words to yourself.

I bet you will start to notice lots of 'youisms', and you will want to change them because they are now so obvious. It's ok we all go through this. And guess what you will also start to notice what others say and do too. That can be quite illuminating. Notice how you feel when you observe friends and family and the things, they repeat out loud.

Journal it: What is your most important person saying to you? What repeated words do you use? What do you notice about your language and what would you like to change?

Changing the script

You know that your mind can program in negative and positive thoughts and beliefs. You know that you have choices. You also know that it takes time. And you know that changing the way that you say or think things changes the script (think of a play) in your mind is amazing. You have the power to reprogram your mind. Because scripts are programs. Running a script, programs and commands your mind to do and behave in a particular way. I am using the word script here because most people watch TV and movies and know that the actors have a script so that they know how to behave. They are following their lines. That's what you do too.

Have you noticed that when you watch a movie, you are affected emotionally when you see certain things? The visuals, sounds and behaviours will trigger you. You might cry at a happy ending or scream in terror when something horrible happens. The scripts create images which trigger feelings and emotions.

Now let's take a book, it has a script, but no pictures. Instead, you create the images in your head, and you feel emotions as you read the words. This is what is happening in your mind. You are running scripts; you will see images and feel emotions and then act in a particular way. This acting forms habits, patterns of thinking and ways of being.

Repeating positive affirmations helps to change the script in your mind so that the book of your life can be rewritten. Imagine what you might change if a movie came on, and you have the power to change the course of action the main players take. Good stuff, eh?

Journal it: What scripts are you running. Write them out and then change them, as you might rewrite the script for a film. How does that feel? What do you learn about yourself?

Visualisation and affirmations

The pictures you see in your mind help you to create visualisations. Visualisations are scripts that people play to imagine great things into place. However, some people believe that because they are not visual, they are unable to 'see' a different future. Pause for a moment and ask -are you Visual / Auditory / Kinaesthetic / Auditory-Digital?

- Visual – see
- Auditory – feel
- Kinaesthetic - feel
- Auditory digital – sense

We can use this in many areas of our life. In this journey, we want to be curious about how we receive and process information so we can make 'visualisation' work for us. Information will come to you in many ways. I, for example, see' images and 'hear' messages in songs, but I also 'feel' others emotions. My primary way is visual. You will also have a primary way, the key is to not overthink visualisation and to use your primary sense so that it works for you.

It is said that information about the external world reaches us via our senses – what we see, hear, touch, smells, taste and sense. One estimate suggests that there is up to two million pieces of information available to us at any one time, so from a very young age, we develop habits of sorting and *re-presenting* that information mentally in our own individual way. Our individual way of thinking and learning is basically our style of perceiving, organising and processing information. But as it's a style that has been practised from a very early age, it will be so familiar to us that it may feel like a fixed part of our personality. Once you accept it's just a style – and that styles can be changed and modified – it opens up the possibility of flexing your style which opens up options to improve the way you think and learn.

Knowing about these styles ensures that you can engage with the wider world, but also know how to make visualisation and affirmations work for you. As always, do what works for you and your mind will do the rest. What if by writing affirmations and saying them created a new script for you to follow and it created wonderful pictures in your mind of how life is, not could be, but is?

Add visualisations to your affirmations. If you say you can do something, see (sense, know, or feel) yourself doing it at the same time. As I have said, I do this while lying in bed in the morning, which sets me up for the day. This helps me to create a clear picture of what I want and how I will feel when my affirmation comes true and a part of me.

When you are ready, you can take a moment to start envisioning the actual outcome of the affirmation. Start to imagine the sights, the sounds, the smells and even the taste of achieving what you want. As you go along, don't forget to feel the emotions you would feel, as if this affirmation was your reality now. Then take daily actions. I always ask what the next aligned step is for this thing to become a reality? And keep it up.

Journal it: Write an affirmation and then write out your visualisation. When you have done this, imagine (see, sense, know or feel) it. Then add – my next aligned step is...

What will happen next?

Usually, as you start to affirm more, your attitude to life will change. You will also notice that as your thoughts change, so do your behaviours and habits. Other people will notice and also change the way that they behave towards you. Be prepared, some may not like the new you, most will adore it, so that's where to focus. Remember your boundaries, protect your energy for the ones that may not like it. Their negative response to you is about them and not you. Plus you have the power of journaling and affirmations to carry you through the day.

When you use affirmations daily, you will notice as well that you will want to declutter your life of things and people that you no longer need. That is also good. When you are surrounded by clutter, it is hard to think. When you get rid of it, new opportunities arrive.

How long does it take?

The answer is some things happen straight away, and some take a bit longer. It took me many years to love myself and think that I was worthy of love. Whereas changing other things was immediate. Stick with it because you are worth it. I have a beautiful affirmation that I use. It's more of a question. Do I love myself enough to? Let's say I want to add in some more self-care, I might ask do I love myself enough to stop work at 2pm for a 40-minute Yoga Nidra? Then my affirmation would be I love myself enough to do a Yoga Nidra every day.

How long does it take? It will take as long as it takes, but the good news is if you stick at it and use your journal to explore what comes up, you will make a difference. What is important is that for this to work, you need to stick with the positive affirmation and not immediately follow it with something negative for the rest of the day. Catch the negatives in your butterfly net and release them back into nature to be grounded and neutralised by Mother Earth.

Affirmation tips

- Keep them short
- Choose words that cannot be seen as negative
- Make them as if they are real – instead of saying I am going to/ I will try - say I am
- Repeat often
- Notice your breath and use your breath to help you relax with the affirmation
- Place your hand on your heart as you say them
- Chose to believe your affirmations
- Enjoy the process and make it fun
- When you have journaled turn what you perceive as a problem into the affirmation for the day
- When you answer a daily journaling prompt end it with an affirmation
- Write today I am and then your affirmation so that it is in the now
- Use your journal to record what happens and remember to celebrate your successes

Affirmations for roots and foundations

- I feel deeply rooted
- My root chakra is balanced
- I am connected to my body
- I feel safe and secure
- I allow myself to feel safe and grounded
- I always feel safe and protected in the world
- I deserve to be safe all the times
- I have a right to be here
- I belong
- I know where I belong, and it is right here
- I allow myself to be nourished and supported by Mother Earth
- I have a juicy life
- I am nourished and hydrated

- I live a nourishing life
- I breathe life in my life
- I am balanced
- All aspects of my life are beautifully balanced
- I am grounded, balanced, stable, and standing on my own two feet
- I am connected with nature
- I am connected with energy, and that energy supports my desires
- I am connected to all that is around me
- I'm always provided for
- I trust that my needs will always be met
- I have what I need
- I see my family through the eyes of love
- My family is happy and healthy
- I always do the best for my family
- I love my beautiful home
- My beautiful home gives me everything I need
- I am attracting an abundance of money
- I accept financial miracles
- I am worthy of financial security
- I am financially free
- I let go of what does not serve me
- I no longer have anything in my life that does not bring me joy
- Letting go is easy

Journal it: Practice writing a few of your own affirmations and try turning them into questions. Remember to add in an aligned action…

110

Gratitude

As we express our gratitude, we must never forget that the highest appreciation is not to utter words but to live by them. John F. Kennedy

After affirmations, I like to add in the practice of gratitude. Combined these help to get you connected to your heart, help you to change perspective and allow you to powerfully reframe your life.

What do you think of when you hear the word gratitude? That you need to be grateful for what you have? Perhaps you see it as a fashionable practice? A way to remember to say thank you for what you have? Something else?

Gratitude is our way of saying thank for something we value, for blessings, miracles and unexpected gifts. It's a feeling that emanates from the heart and therefore from a place of love. It helps you to connect with spirit, divine inner wisdom and consciousness. It also keeps you grounded in the real world.

Every culture in the world has a word for thank you. It is often a word that we take for granted. Consider when you go for a meal, and the waiter or waitress places your food in front of you, I assume you would automatically say thank you. Just as you would if someone held a door open. What about when you receive a gift?

Gratitude is saying thank you and appreciating your gifts, no matter where these come from. They could be innate gifts that you take for granted, e.g. the way that your body knows how to heal, the gifts from Mother Nature, gifts of kindness from friends and strangers, the gift of love from your dogs, a present for your birthday, and any gift that arrives unexpectedly.

Gratitude is a feeling that comes from the heart and reaches all parts of your body. Of course, it is also a choice, you can choose to be grateful for what you have, or you can take it for granted and assume you will always have it – but you wouldn't do that, would you?

Gratitude is an attitude – a way of being where you do not take things for granted, and it shows up in the way that you are. Gratitude creates connections – within and with everything around you. It strengthens the bond you have with your mind, body, spirit and soul and with others that you meet. It creates a powerful energetic resonance.

What do you notice about the way your life changes when you express gratitude for what you have? What do you notice about others? Can you even tell if someone practices gratitude? People who practice gratitude are often generous and the kind of people who do things like random acts of kindness without any expectation of getting something back. I think what I notice about others is that they seem to be humble, kind, generous, content and have an air of inner peace.

What is appreciation?

Many of us use the words gratitude and appreciation interchangeably.

- Gratitude is about saying thank you, a feeling and an attitude
- Appreciation is acknowledging the perceived value for what you get and the meaning you place on the gift. It's where you create a positive emotional connection

The way that I look at it is that I say I am grateful and then feel appreciation. I am grateful that I awaken to the birds singing and am able to see a glorious sunrise. I appreciate the beauty of Mother Earth and know that I am lucky to live in a beautiful part of the world.

You may find that you feel grateful for something and may not appreciate it. Let's consider the body, you may be thankful for what it does to support you without fully acknowledging that from the tiniest cell that every tissue, organ and system is finely calibrated to keep you moving, healthy and alive.

You can be grateful for the food on your table and then take it a step further and appreciate the person who prepared it, the flavour and nutritional value and how that supports a healthy body.

When thinking of appreciation, consider the value that something provides and what value you get from it. When you know the source of your gratitude, you will start to fully appreciate what is available to you.

What is a gratitude practice?

Practising gratitude starts by paying attention and taking the time to notice what is going on. When you wake in the morning, how do you feel about the quality of the sleep that you experienced? What about the gorgeous breakfast or the shower that was magically just the right temperature? What about when you look at your face in the mirror do you feel grateful that the person looking back at you got you to this point? As you emerge from the house and look up into the morning sky, do you behold it in wonder?

Gratitude, along with appreciation, helps you to cultivate a meaningful framework for life and the gifts that you receive. Everything is a gift, even the rubbish stuff because through every experience you learn something and through that learning can make conscious choices.

The practise of gratitude helps you to develop a conscious connection with everything. Imagine that you are ill, and by practising gratitude, your body responds and heals quickly. What about if you find yourself lost and someone goes out of their way to show you the way you need to go, or they help you out if you find yourself in a not too favourable situation.

What are the benefits of practising gratitude?

- Creates strong foundations for all areas of your life
- Increased happiness, contentment and positive mood
- Less toxic, negative emotions that could cause a physical impact on the body
- A sense of inner peace
- More satisfaction with life
- Less materialistic
- Better able to deal with stress

- Better health
- Better sleep
- Greater resiliency
- Encourages the development of kindness, patience, humility, and wisdom
- Helps you to manifest magic and bring more abundance into your life

Practising gratitude creates contentment, inner peace and compassion

When you are grounded, connected with Mother Earth, content and find yourself in a place of inner peace, you will feel greater compassion for yourself and others. As a consequence, you will attract the right people and things into your life. Best of all is the development of self-love. The Dalai Lama says: "If you don't love yourself, you cannot love others. If you have no compassion for yourself, then you are not capable of developing compassion for others."

What gratitude does is create the right foundations and environment for you be the best version of you. When you put yourself first, learn to love and appreciate all that you are and have, you build a pot of energy from which you can fuel and nurture yourself. If you don't have a bucket full of love and energy for yourself, how will you be able to support others or live your best life – on purpose and with meaning?

What I learned was that gratitude and appreciation for how my body knew how to heal given the right ingredients, gave me back my life. I had worked on loving myself before having fractures, so that helped and supported my healing process. It is with this knowledge that I continue to reap the rewards of this practice.

Gratitude transforms your past, present and future

Gratitude has changed my life, and it can change yours too. As you focus on being grateful, it will help you to reframe that past so that you see things differently. It's about understanding that life happens for you, not to you and to thank you for these gifts. This will enable you to be more in the present. As you reframe life from the perspective of gratitude, the way that you approach the future will change. I am sure that when you reflect back, you will notice incredible learning.

When you focus on how far you have travelled rather than dwelling on the bad stuff, you will find life far more rewarding. When you see a progression, you will feel better about yourself. This will encourage you to go forward again.

The way that each of us remembers the past and encodes it is very personal and therefore our ability to see these incidents and gain perspective will be different to someone else. One person may make quicker progress, and that may be because they have been working of themselves in other ways and practising gratitude for longer than you. Everyone will progress at the right rate for them.

In moving forward, it's not just practising gratitude that will help you to progress, you may find that you need to work on boundaries, forgiveness, self-love and other things as well. The good news is as you work out what you need to do and focus on being grateful for the gifts you have been given, you will progress and change how you feel about your past and the opportunities that your future presents.

When the past is viewed through a different lens, this will change how you live in the present moment. I like to see the past as a set of experiences that fuels me to be a better person. These memories are like an encyclopaedia, rather than a place to dwell. The events of the past inspire me to live my best life every day. How you remember your past is your choice, you can focus on the pain or the learning that you have gained.

My past was pretty messy and not pleasant, and I do occasionally slip into anger and shame, but not for long. I look at what comes up and ask myself why now and what do I need to learn? Where are the gifts and how can I can grow from this? From this position, I can design how I live today and how I move into my tomorrows.

There are always going to challenges and stuff that comes along to knock your confidence and dreams, but once again how you view these things will help you to reframe and make better choices about what you are going to do.

To fully enjoy being in the now, you need to appreciate what you have. Gratitude in the now is all about appreciating fully what you have. When you wake in the morning, what do you think about? If you took a moment to appreciate where you are, and what you have, how would that set your day up? Ask yourself, how do I want this day to go? And how would I like to feel?

Imagine starting your day affirming and acknowledging all of the beauty within you and around you. Imagine acknowledging that you are an amazing person with fabulous skills and experiences to share, how would that change how you approach your day?

What if you knew that you could have a gorgeous day today and every day by focusing on what you could create, by appreciating what you have. We are in charge of where we are going, even though it may not always feel like it. It's our life, our story and our choice about how we create the world in which we live and love.

What if you were already grateful for the future to come? We know that visualisation is powerful. So, if you added gratitude for the future to come, how would that be? Can you imagine what experiences you want to have and how you would like to feel? By being grateful today and reframing yesterday, you have the ability to consciously create a future that you will love.

How not to practice gratitude

Make it an enjoyable practice, and don't try too hard. Constructing massive lists and always being appreciative might get a little overwhelming. You may also feel resentful if you are extending gratitude to someone who isn't worthy. Consider any unhelpful or toxic relationships that you may want to let go off. Be grateful for the lesson, let go and let love.

Stop and think for a moment if you are the kind of person to downplay your success and achievements. Remember to own your greatness while saying thank you to others for supporting you. You can express gratitude AND take appropriate credit for your own successes.

And finally, not all situations are worthy of gratitude and appreciation. Be true to your heart and show up in an authentic way. Remember, gratitude is a feeling that comes into the heart.

What to expect

What should you expect to experience as you practice gratitude? Here are a few things to consider:
- It may feel like a chore. That's the same with lots of things, and if you don't stick to it you will never feel the benefits

- It will take time until you start to notice the benefits. This will vary from person to person. The more you practice, the stronger the feelings and benefits become
- At first, you may notice some negative stuff coming in. This is normal. Observe what is happening, explore and reflect. Over time more positive emotions will be the norm
- Eventually, you will look at life differently, and your attitude to others will change

How gratitude changes you and your brain

We are all sculptors of our own mind and body. The mind is an incredible creation and one, which we are only just beginning to understand, despite years of research. It is both highly adaptable and flexible in more ways than we can fathom. Yet we only scratch the surface of its capabilities.

Most of our primary functions are governed by our subconscious. When it comes to movement, for example, our brain sends out messages along our nerves to various muscles in our bodies in order to perform specific functions. With repetition, the network of neurons in our brains become efficient at learning how to do the things that we habitually do – so habits are formed. When you learn something new, the old pathways can become redundant as new routes are created. Which is why we have the phrase use it or lose it. And, of course, there may be pathways that we'd rather forget.

As we go through our days, our minds and bodies are continually tweaking and making thousands of adjustments, to make the best possible decision in any given situation. As you experience slowing it down, getting connected to you and practising gratitude your neurological pathways rewire.

The brain is like any muscle it needs training if we want it to perform in a particular way. By practising gratitude, you get into a flow state of conscious love and connection. The new thoughts that you have will create new realities. We are not our thoughts, but by choosing a new life menu, we are taking responsibility for a new mindset and trusting that when the food of life arrives, it will be truly delicious.

You can change lifelong habits and unhelpful thoughts within a few days. Naturally, it will take time for the practice and attitude of gratitude to kick in but kick in it will. Our subconscious will make the necessary changes if allowed to. That means as you start your gratitude practice, you may notice intruding thoughts. If you observe these without judgement, allowing them to be neither right nor wrong, you will find that they will change.

As your practice develops, you will design an internal code for your values, beliefs, habits and behaviours. When you explore your future from an as if state you are creating visions which your mind will be happy to investigate. Imagery is the preferred language of our subconscious. Give it a vision, and it will do miraculous things to bring it into being.

Most great things in your life will have started with a dream, something that you want to create. But life gets in the way. Practising daily gratitude and envisioning fuels our future plans. The key is to keep practising otherwise like a plant that isn't watered your dreams will wither and die.

If we stay true to our vision, continuously taking the path that best aligns with it, and put in the hard work, keep focused on what you are grateful for and will be grateful for, nature will take its course, and our visions will soon become our reality.

I believe humans are always in pursuit of bettering themselves. That often means that we might forget to celebrate our successes and achievements. Gratitude is a way of celebrating. When you acknowledge your accomplishments and state what you are thankful for your mind will know what to go after – the good stuff. This will naturally keep you motivated to do more. This gives you purpose and a reason to be.

Celebrating strengthens our positive intention towards continuing the same behaviour. It is an important part of our living our best lives.

We hear of spiritual leaders, musicians, writers, actor and athletes all being connected and inflow when performing. Connection isn't just for the chosen few. When you practice gratitude, you will find that you are connected to a deeper part of you that wants to flow love around your body and out into the world. The truth is that you have always been connected, you just didn't notice.

When you remain in gratitude, amazing things will happen. Your health will improve, as will your relationships, you'll feel more grounded and connected to your heart, inner wisdom and to the people and things around you.

Being thankful for every moment will open a gateway to your higher self, your spirituality and consciousness. Enjoy every second as you meet your greatest self.

Life is not a dress rehearsal. You are alive and on this beautiful planet for such a small period of time, so why not cherish every day as if it is your last? There is no greater gift or anything more valuable than the value of each day. If you change your focus from doing to being, you will open up to more opportunities and probably more fun, as well as discovering inner peace and contentment.

Journal it: Now it's your turn, take a few moments to reflect on the last few months of your life. What are you grateful for? Big or small, it doesn't matter, simply write and reflect.

Gratitude journaling magic

Gratitude turns what we have into enough. Anonymous

Giving thanks makes you happy. Journaling helps to create change. Bring them both together, and that is the amazing power of word alchemy. When you write about what you appreciate, there is a vibration that is carried to the page. Try writing and then moving your hands over the words. I wonder what you will sense? Try it again by saying what you are grateful for, how does that change the energy for you? Gratitude journaling creates a magical vibrational energy that flows throughout your being and out into the world.

Your gratitude journal

As you go about your day, engage your five senses as often as possible so that you become aware of the things you can feel grateful for and appreciate. Then take a moment to be present to each element as you notice it and become aware of your feelings. Also go deeper and fully understand what has been made available to you. Remember your affirmation and reflect on this. When it comes to gratitude, write anything from the mundane, material to the magnificent, while focusing on the heart chakra area – also remember to connect to your roots.

Challenges and lessons

What challenges and lessons came up from the things you felt gratitude for. In writing this, it will open your awareness to the deeper meaning of gratitude.

Gifts

What gifts did the things you are grateful for, plus the challenges and lesson? Why do you consider them to be gifts?

Appreciation

Remember to consider the source of your gratitude and appreciate the abundance that is coming into your life. Regular gratitude and appreciation will rev up your energy and help you to create a more loving and fulfilling life.

Journal it: When you begin your gratitude practice recall what you have noticed during the day or week. When you are ready, write at least three things that you are grateful for stated in the present tense. State I am grateful for... For example:

- I am grateful that it is safe to love me
- I am grateful that I am surrounded by beautiful and loving friends and family
- I am grateful for my healthy boundaries and kind heart

When you have finished writing what you are grateful for breath in love from your root chakra, up your body and into your heart and connect to your appreciation.

The roots of your gratitude

When you start your gratitude practice, consider the roots of your gratitude. Take a few moments to connect to what you are grateful for and follow the pathway or story. You will be fascinated by what comes up. It's important as you follow the roots to stay out of the story and to become a witness to what you observe. You may see, feel or sense memories, images, feelings, sounds, smells or tastes. Make a note and use them to learn from. As you consider what you are grateful for you can also focus on what you need day to day in order to survive and thrive. When you feel grounded and safe, you will feel confident that the Universe is fully supporting your needs.

The heart of your gratitude

Next, bring your heart into your gratitude practice. It's important as you connect with your heart, as this will enable your heart to open and to fully feel appreciation. You can do this with the three hearts meditation (The alchemy of the breath and meditations) Take as long as you like. When you feel connected, you can start to write about what you are grateful for today. When you have finished writing what you are grateful for, breathe out love from your heart.

As you become comfortable with connecting with the roots and heart of your gratitude, start exploring your gratitude in a more curious way. By that I mean, perhaps take a bit more time to notice, or have a few more conversations with your heart, play with the energy and have fun.

Remember to combine your gratitude practice with any of the other practices described.

I don't have to chase extraordinary moments to find happiness - it's right in front of me if I'm paying attention and practising gratitude.

Brene Brown

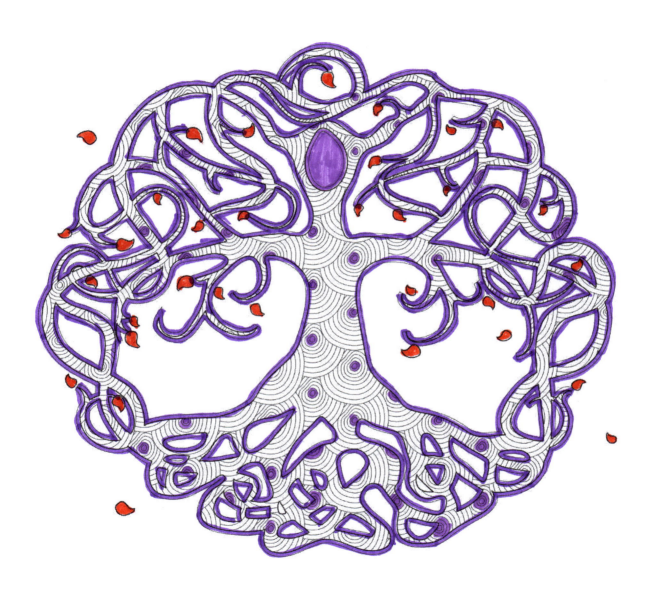

Roots and foundations journaling prompts

I am grounded and centred

Over the next few chapters, you will learn more about your roots and foundations. In each of the chapters, you will find a set of prompts that you can use for inspiration. You could pick an area and work on that for the week or pick a prompt that resonates on the day. Perhaps you could choose a mandala with an affirmation to focus on first. To get more out of your journaling, you could follow up with what you are grateful for and the gratitude process.

The root chakra is about our basic needs for:

- Safety and security
- Trust
- Belonging
- Home
- Family
- Money, abundance and prosperity
- Physical health and wellbeing (nourishment)
- Stability (balance)

When this chakra is balanced

- You will feel safe and secure in yourself
- Grounded in reality and common sense
- Feel like you belong
- Feel at home in your environment and your body
- Know how to create a healthy life
- Feel abundant, prosperous and respect money
- Have great foundations to manifest what you want in life
- Can easily create order and structure

Unbalanced and not in the flow

- Fearful and anxious
- Fear of change
- Lack of focus
- Do not trust yourself or others
- Self-destructive
- Home and family life is in a mess

- Finances are neglected
- Poor or rigid boundaries
- Eating habits awry – e.g. over or undereat or eat emotionally
- Unstructured

Focus on your roots and foundations

Our root chakra helps us to feel fully rooted and grounded here on Earth. Have you ever looked at a tree? I am sure you have. Trees stand tall because of their healthy root system and grow towards the sky, where it has space to breathe. The roots on a tree bring nutrients and water to feed and nourish it. Which, in turn, helps it to grow. By creating strong roots, the tree has a robust foundation to help it withstand the storms of life. When your roots are strong, you can anchor yourself, and with the right nourishment reach towards the heavens to be anything you want.

Under the roots of all trees is the heart of Mother Earth. This is the place of beginnings. It is where you begin your journey to discovering you, creating strong roots and foundations to carry you through life.

Trees carry incredible wisdom and embedded deeply in their trunks are the circles and cycles of life, which tell the stories of many beginnings and endings. Like us, they have grown from the seeds planted by their family before them and like them, you pass on the knowledge you gain through this lifetime to your family and others.

As a tree grows, so do you, tall and standing in your power. Trees offer lots of support to the world around them – shelter, food, safety, air and shade. Their energy brings balance and groundedness.

Everyone has roots and beginnings, stories of how you became who you are. Stories that bring you to where you now find yourselves. By exploring your stories, you can trace the beginnings of them, let go of what no longer serves you and use your wisdom to empower and propel yourself forward.

As the cycles of your life change, so will the nature of your roots. At each stage of life, you will be planting seeds, birthing, growing, letting go and dying. You'll be chopping away the deadwood to make way for what is needed in the next part of your adventure.

This pruning will make your tree stronger. As you eliminate dead wood, you are leaving space for new growth. At the root chakra, it's essential to let go of old beliefs and maybe possessions, so that you only have what nurtures you.

Curiously delving in memories enables you to make sense, but to also move forward. It is when you can find gifts in the stories and being grateful for the learning that you become wise.

As trees stand together in community, supporting each other, so must humans. Everyone is connected by the vast root system that is humanity. By first establishing your roots, feeling safe, secure and strong, you can then move forward to build a better life for you and for those you love and whose lives you can touch.

Appreciate your inner wisdom, and by accessing it through your root system, you can gain a deeper understanding of who you are and your path. You can also find new or better ways of communicating with others and feeling a sense of belonging.

By strengthening your roots and foundations through the practice of gratitude, honouring your past, present and future, you can walk your chosen path through life with purpose and meaning.

Your first chakra and your roots and foundations

This first chakra helps you to create a strong, secure and stable base from which to live your life and grow into your best self. The root chakra is made up of whatever you need to ground you to stability in your life. This includes your basic needs such as food, water, shelter, safety, as well as your emotional needs of interconnection and belonging. When these needs are met, you feel *grounded and safe*. When you are at odds with these needs, life can spiral out of control, and you can often feel overwhelmed by your thoughts, and you can become ungrounded.

In the body, the root chakra is found at the base of the spine, and one of its roles is to look after the bones. Just like the trunk of a tree, your spine is the foundation of your body, holding you in your power. If there is a crack in your foundations, then the rest of your life may feel a little wobbly, too. When your roots and foundations are healthy and well-nourished, you will feel safe, secure, well balanced, grounded, empowered, and confident.

When I think about roots, I think about the experiences that have brought me to this point – the origins of who I am today, some of which have been great gifts and other challenges. As I tackle my challenges and appreciate the gifts from the lessons, life does indeed feel sweeter.

By having deep roots just like the tree, you can grow on many levels, which gives you the courage and strength to tackle anything. A tree will send its roots deep into the soil, looking for the right nutrients to grow strong. If you have ever noticed a root system, they are never straight. A tree sends its roots in many directions seeking only the best and weaving them together to develop an incredible support infrastructure – its foundation. To create this balance, we need to reconnect to the heart of Mother Earth on every level.

What does being grounded mean?

You will often hear people talking about being grounded while working with the root chakra. Being grounded is about feeling connected to you and having a connection with the present moment. When you are grounded and open to the Universe, you become a channel for Universal energy to move through you. You have your roots in reality and feel connected to everything around you. You feel the earth firmly beneath your feet. When you're grounded, you are aware of and in control of your emotional, spiritual and mental state and needs. Often when the crown chakra is open, and someone's head is in the clouds, grounding will bring them back to earth.

People also talk about being centred alongside being grounded. Imagine that you feel secure, stable and in the present moment and something throws you off. Centring means coming back to a space inside of your heart that anchors you in the moment, helping you to catch your breath and bring you into a place of inner peace. You can also think of it as coming into your heart space so that you can balance your mind, body and spirit.

One way I ground and centre myself is to imagine that roots are growing from my feet going into Mother Earth while placing one hand on my belly and focusing on my breath.

My breath is rooted in the heart of Mother Earth, and she keeps me grounded

Timelines and turning points

The map of my life reveals incredible experiences

The timelines and turning points exercise is a perfect place to begin the journey to uncovering the memories in your root chakra. We use timelines and turning points to help us examine the past. We are looking for clues and connection to possibilities and opportunities that might not otherwise seem obvious. Timelines help us to discover locked away thoughts, memories, skills, talents, and experiences, which go to make up your stories. Their value comes from **observing and reflecting** on what has been captured on your visual storyboard. When you stand back and observe your life, you will gain a lot of clarity. You also need to be prepared to keep walking away to reflect, coming back and trying to see what is missing or what needs moving around. You are looking for patterns, connections, and themes.

Why timelines are so powerful

Timelines are powerful because they are a storyboard, a pictorial representation and humans see things in patterns. It really is as simple as that. The powerful part comes in taking time to stand back and reflect. To let your unconscious mind go into flow and make the connections. When you do this using visually using colour, your story comes alive. Even if you are a person who says I am a logical left-brainer, let me stop you. You have two sides of your brain and regardless of how you want to pigeon hole yourself as a 'list kind of person', your brain will do what it wants, and it will use all of its processing power, right side – the big picture, left side - detail and connections.

This exercise will enable you to uncover the book of your life, so hold that in your intention.

How to create a timeline

Start brainstorming

- Get a large sheet of paper
- You are going to create a timeline (chakra years) across the top and themes (life areas) along one side
    - Root chakra 0-7
    - Sacral chakra 8-14
    - Solar plexus chakra 15-21
    - Heart chakra 22-28
    - Throat chakra 29-35
    - Third eye chakra 36-42
    - Crown chakra 43.49
- Armed with post-it notes of a variety of colours and coloured pens/pencils, put your date of birth at one end and today's date at the far end
- Next, divide your timeline into blocks of seven years (chakras)
- Along the side put in the life areas-
    - Health and wellbeing
    - Learning
    - Financial
    - Heart and spirit
    - Experiences
    - Mental/emotional
    - Love/Partner
    - Family
    - Friends
    - Mission/Vision
- Start brainstorming.
- As you look at the themes and time zones, let thoughts come into your mind without censorship

- As a thought comes to mind put it on a post-it and place it where you consider it should go for now. You might use similar colours for certain thoughts or ideas
- When you have brainstormed, take some time out
- Later reflect on what you have written, move things around and add more, do not get rid of any
- When you are ready, start looking for connections, themes and aha moments
- Consider how your developmental years have impacted your personal growth
- Use coloured pens to mark up how each experience maps to a chakra. So for example, if you have highlighted that you have money issues, then this would be in red to indicate that it comes from the root chakra
- Use your journal to write about what comes up

Once you can see the connections, you will be able to see where your life themes are. For example, things that happened in childhood may have created a lack of self-worth as an adult, which in turn has meant that you have always settled for mediocre jobs, rather than becoming an entrepreneur. Health issues could be as a direct result of emotional pain from actions or inactions. Poor relationships maybe a relentless search for someone like (or unlike) your father. Your inability to write and publish a book could be linked to self-worth around being told you were a rubbish speller.

Once you have completed your timelines exercise, which you will do as you work with each chakra, in this case, the root chakra, you are ready for turning points.

Turning points

This is another exercise that I like to do with lots of reflection in-between. Please take your time. What will happen is that once you have started your unconscious mind will continue in its flow state and keep throwing things at you.

Examining the past can be upsetting, especially when you look back and see a set of repeated behaviours that might now seem cringeworthy. I like to think that despite everything that has happened, it was all meant to be and is just part of the journey, like a tough degree programme at the University of Life. Everything is a learning experience.

- Go back to your timeline and start looking for turning points
- Make a note of each of these ensuring that they stand out

Next, take each of your turning points and do the following.

- Using your journal, create a page (or two) for every turning point
- On each sheet answer the turning point questions below, you can add your own, but for now, let's keep it simple
- Look for points at which you changed direction or made important, potentially life-changing decisions or points at which change was thrust on you
- Look for times of personal and spiritual growth

Turning point questions

- Describe your life at this time?
- What did you learn that contributed to your spiritual and personal growth?
- What were the gifts and lessons?
- How have these empowered you to be a better person, and how have these helped you to help others?

Your life file

At the end of the writing period, you will have a 'life' file. This file is useful for when you feel stuck in the journaling process and looking at the roots of the root chakra areas. When you understand what got you here, good and not so good, you have the knowledge to support you moving forward.

Roots and feeling safe

I always feel safe and protected in the world

The bodies natural call is to keep you safe, and this is fundamental to your wellbeing. You will have heard of flight, fright or freeze. This is where your brain decides what the best course of action is when it is faced with a perceived threat. For example, you may get triggered to use one of these responses when you feel unsafe or rejected, your finances are not stable, you are in a caught in a conflict, or when old feelings are surfaced when you face a similar situation from the past. What is important is to know what feeling safe means to you, and to know when you are heading for an emotional hijacking. Then understanding what you can do about it. Notice what happens in your body and work to ground and centre yourself.

You may not be able to stop your emotions flaring up and from reacting to a perceived threat, but you can be aware of your physical state, your internal thoughts and respond productively. One way is to consider your own unproductive response from a past situation and replace it with a productive one. You'll become more aware of these through journaling and reflective writing. Think of the tree again and how, when it has strong roots, it is unlikely to be ripped up from the ground and toppled over.

Journaling prompts

- What is one thing right now that will help you to feel more secure?
- What fearful thoughts are stopping you from feeling safe?

- What are some fears you have around my safety and security that you are not letting go of? Ask why?
- List all of your fears around feeling safe. Next, write down all of the beautiful things that would happen if you were able to overcome these
- What limiting beliefs about your safety and security are holding you back, and what can you do to reframe these?
- How are your basic needs around feeling safe being taken care of? If they are not, what can you do?
- Do you feel supported? If not, why not? And how can you improve this?
- Who are the people that make you feel unsafe? What can you do about them?
- What are the situations that make you feel unsafe? What can you do about them?
- Where in your life could you set stronger boundaries so that you feel more secure in who you are and your life?
- Spell out SAFE and make each letter form a random word. Then freewrite for 10 minutes

Roots and trust

I trust in my choices and decisions

There are so many reasons why we don't trust ourselves. Trust is about belief, and it is how we act when we either trust ourselves and others or not. It is also tied to confidence. When you do not trust yourself or others, then naturally you become fearful of what you might do or say.

Have you noticed that when someone does something to you that breaks your trust that this becomes difficult to shake off when you find yourself in a similar situation? This can be particularly true of relationships where perhaps your partner has been unfaithful and subsequently, it is difficult to trust them or others not to do this to you again.

What about when it comes to eating, can you trust yourself to not eat the whole packet of biscuits or to just eat one chunk of chocolate? Or perhaps you don't venture out of your comfort zone because you don't trust that you can do whatever is required?

If lack of trust in anything is plaguing you, then you could find that some of the joy goes out of life because you become too fearful of committing to something. And then, of course, that old rogue self-sabotage could show up to hold you back even more.

The problem is that this lack of trust is operating at a level that you are not even aware of. The first place, therefore, to address this is becoming aware of your behaviour. Do not judge it, simply acknowledge that this is what you have been doing. Tracing the roots will help you to understand where and when this first started, and from there, you can decide that you want to learn to trust again.

Self-trust is like anything it needs the practice to get into the muscle. Make a decision that you will commit to trusting again. You might affirm that you are always on the right path. Trust that your goals lead you somewhere and that the right way is continually unfolding.

Creating healthy boundaries and learning to say no will ensure that you can protect yourself until such time you want to go beyond your comfort zone. Be vulnerable and give it a go, sometimes you have to let your guard down and trust all will be well. You can practice showing your vulnerability in a safe setting. Talk to a close family member or good friend and be open with them about how you are feeling.

The bottom line is that to trust others, you have to trust yourself first and in your ability to make good choices. Even if someone has hurt you, this is not because you failed or made a mistake, this is down to them and their behaviour. If you can understand their motivations, then this will help you to know why. Of course, the same applies to you, what were your reasons for not trusting? This is where trusting your intuition comes in. Do you listen to your gut feelings or your heart? Listening and trusting your intuition will guide you through life.

Look at all of the things that you do trust and all of the great decisions you did make and do more of these. In this way, you will build your trust muscle. Consider relationships you ended because of broken trust or things you tried and succeeded at. What does that tell you? What else can you look at- career, financial, health or friendships? All of this is a great reminder that you are in tune with yourself.

Forgive and let go, holding onto what happened is not healthy. Take a look at roots and letting go there is a wonderful forgiveness process there. In addition to forgiveness, allow yourself to grieve any losses. You may be mourning the end of a relationship that wasn't healthy or a life you knew that wasn't serving you. Grief is the emotion at the heart chakra, and this is where working with your heart on self-love is essential to your healing. Allow yourself to feel these emotions and use your journal to help you to process them. Finally, leave the past behind and set your expectations for a life where you trust, respect and honour yourself.

Trust journaling prompts

- What does trust mean to you?
- How would trusting yourself help to improve the quality of your life?

- How much do you trust others? Do you trust everyone, some people or no one? Can you pinpoint why?
- Do you have issues relying on others and believe that you can only trust yourself?
- Do you feel vulnerable around others so that you don't trust yourself to commit to something? When this happens, what are you thinking or feeling? How can you reframe this?
- Do you listen to your gut feelings or your heart when making decisions?
- What are your motivations for not trusting yourself? How can you reframe these?
- Make a list of the good choices you made and remind yourself how strong your instincts are
- How can you forgive those that have betrayed or hurt you?
- How can you forgive yourself for decisions and choices that didn't support you?
- Spell TRUST and make each letter form a random word. Then freewrite for 10 minutes.

Trust in yourself and your dreams

Roots and belonging

I know where I belong, and it is right here

The root chakra is also about belonging to a tribe or a group. And this is how we create connection. Because as humans, we want to be connected to a community. This gives us social wealth.

Belonging is such an essential human need. Not to just belong but to be accepted for who you are. Your identity is tied into this feeling of belonging and covers what you have in common or what differentiates you from others. What is important is being grateful for everything that you are, honouring and appreciating everything about you. From the moment we are born, we want to belong to some kind of group or community. Mostly that's going to start with family. And then other aspects of belonging will grow.

As we get older, we want to be included by others. There's nothing worse than feeling rejected, and we want to feel accepted by society. Everyone has some kind of experience of belonging or not belonging. You might have a really lovely, delicious, close-knit family. And you feel that you belong at every social gathering.

Conversely, you might be the black sheep of the family. And every time you go to a gathering, it's like, Oh no, he or she's turned up. You may find yourself amused by that, but you may find yourself feeling rejected by those people. You could end up feeling anger and frustration and maybe confused.

You might feel like you belong in your close family, but you might feel that you don't belong in your extended family. You might feel that you belong when you're with a certain friend, but when those friends bring other friends in suddenly, you don't feel part of it. You feel like they're all kind of cliquey and you're not part of the gang, and you don't feel close to them. You feel uncomfortable, and you just want to get away as quickly as possible.

In groups, often you feel like you have a common identity. Think about some of the social groups that you are in – family, a relationship, jobs, social gatherings, circles, clubs, memberships, all sorts of things. When you're in the social groups, what characteristics do they have, and why do you feel that you belong? How does belonging feel?

Social groups are about belonging as a whole. When you belong to a group that might be part of how you identify yourself. I'm in a spiritual book club because I read spiritual books and you might identify yourself as part of that. What's also interesting about social groups is they often adopt the same kind of dress, similar mannerisms and things like that. You might do that to fit in with the rest of the group, because this not only helps you to feel like you belong, it also helps you to feel safe.

When you're in a group, there's loads and loads of benefits, like shared values and interests and shared beliefs. Being part of a group really promotes this sense of wellbeing and happiness. Research shows that when you are in a group where you are accepted and loved, that helps you to grow as a person. And we do feel a lot happier.

How do you connect with the people that are in the group? And what do you learn about yourself? You might find it really, really hard to go to networking meetings because you find it really difficult to connect to strangers. What does that teach you about you? What can you do about it?

You may need to declutter groups that you are in. Maybe when we lose our job, people that we worked with are no longer our friends, because we don't see them anymore and grow apart. Or what about when you decide that the religion that you've been following is not part of who you are anymore. Perhaps you go from being in a spiritualist church to a Christian environment or the other way around, or you've been in a cult, and now you go to a different church.

As well as benefits there are lots of downsides. For example, when you are rejected. You will experience a whole range of emotions that come up, and they are good to explore. When you are excluded from belonging in a group, what comes up? What does being excluded mean to you? What does that tell you about your roots? Do you cling on to a group because you don't want to be alone? Do you cling onto a group because that takes away who you are?

These are some great things to explore in your journal, and all of this can be traced all the way back to something that is potentially unresolved as a child. When you explore where do those roots of belonging take you?

Is there a particular environment in which you feel like you belong? That might be family or where you work. It might be a club or a membership or a group. It could equally be outside on the beach, in the mountains. Perhaps you love cities. They give you a sense of belonging. Where do you feel like you belong? I, for example, I love the countryside. If I go to a bustling city, it's horrible. I hate it. There's too much noise and too many people. I feel like I just want to get away or escape. Other people, for example, might find the ocean and the crashing waves and that vast emptiness completely disturbing. What environments do you feel like you belong or don't you feel like you belong?

Belonging in your body is something people don't often associate with belonging. It means being present and alive to sensations, feelings, energy and experiences. When you think about it, your body is the first home of your own. It is the home of you, your spirit and your soul. Its where you live every day and where you carry the stories of every experience. Yet, so many people feel disconnected from their bodies, and this might be through negative life experiences. Through healing practices which includes journaling and things like yoga, meditation, hydration and nourishment, you can come home to your body. When you start to practice gratitude and appreciation for your body, you will begin to feel safe and at home in your body.

Journaling prompts

- What does belonging mean to you?
- What comes up when you explore belonging?
- Create a clear picture of what belonging means to you, describe what you see in detail
- When you feel like you don't belong what comes up for you? Is there a pattern?
- Which kind of groups do you feel you most belong to and why?
- What do you love and appreciate most about the groups you belong in?
- What do you notice about how you behave in groups? What does this teach you?
- Is there a particular environment where you feel like you belong? Family/Place of work/Club/It could be the beach, the mountains, open fields, bustling cities, deserts, and so forth

- Where do you feel that you don't belong? Family/Place of work/Club/It could be the beach, the mountains, open fields, bustling cities, deserts, and so forth
- How can you ensure that you belong where you want to?
- What three things could you do so that you feel like you belong in your body?
- Spell BELONG and make each letter form a random word. Then freewirte for 10 minutes

Roots and home

I love my beautiful home

Your home (outside of your body) should be somewhere you enjoy spending time. A personal space that brings you peace and relaxation, especially after a long day at work. To support your root chakra, make your home a sacred space that welcomes you as soon as you walk in the door. Your home environment should be a sanctuary and an area where you can recharge and feel nourished. The energetic signature of everyone that has ever lived your house is held there just as it holds your energy as well. Our homes are also an extension of who we are and how we express ourselves.

Maybe for you home, isn't a place. Maybe it's a feeling. Home might be a place where your memories lie. My home is a place where I feel safe. I love my home, and I feel very safe and secure here. I don't have to hide who I am, but also I think of home as where my heart is.

Home is a part of who you are just by definition because when you think about how you decorate your house or perhaps how you do your garden, that is an expression of your identity, but also your home is maybe your roots and your memories, a place where you grew up. Perhaps you have fond memories or maybe not such fond memories.

The colours of the rooms in your home are a direct reflection of your personality. Room colour can influence our moods and our thoughts. Red will raise a room's energy. It often works as an accent colour in the living or dining room and is probably not a great idea for a bedroom. Earthy tones, on the other hand, tend to be calming and peaceful. Have a look around your home and think about how it identifies who you are.

I don't live in my country of birth, but where I live is my home. When I go back to see my friends, I say, I'm going home, which is crazy, because this is my home, I say it because there is a sense of familiarity and belonging. Are you strongly connected to a particular place? When I think of where I have lived and my homes, there isn't a strong connection. I am not connected to my place at birth, either. My father was in the RAF, so we travelled, I didn't have anywhere that I could call a proper home for many, many years. We just moved and moved and moved. Home is now where I feel safe and secure, and where I have an anchor, a place to be myself.

Declutter your home

Lots of clutter in your home will drag you and your energy down. I can't stand seeing piles of stuff everywhere, and I hate a messy desk. However, I know it's easy to let things pile up around the house, especially during the week when you're tired after work. If too much clutter in your home creates a block in the flow in energy, then it makes sense to declutter. Get rid of everything that doesn't add value to your home and life. Take your time and tackle a room at a time.

The root is particularly connected to two rooms, the kitchen and toilet. The kitchen because food sustains and nourishes us and the toilet because that's where we eliminate what we don't need. A third space would be a basement, cellar or any area that sits at the bottom of the house. Keep this clear, and it will ensure that the energy is clear for the rest of your home.

To stay in flow with this chakra, declutter the kitchen and get rid of food that is old or is not so good for you. Make it a place where you enjoy cooking and eating. In the bathroom, make sure the pipes are flowing, and it's a place where you enjoy taking a bath. The basement is often the place where everything gets dumped, make sure you clear it up.

Support your root chakra by making your home a place where you feel safe, secure, balanced and harmonious and most of all, a place where your heart is. And of course, feeling grateful and full of appreciation for everything your home provides for you.

Journaling prompts

- Explore. What does home mean to you? Is it a place, a feeling, a memory or somewhere you currently live? Does it give you safety and security?
- Is home your place of birth? Do you feel very strongly connected to that? Is this where your heart is?
- When you are home, do you feel that you can be who you want to be?
- Do you feel safe in your home environment? If not, why not, and what can you do to improve this?
- What five things do you love and appreciate about your home?
- How does coming home make you feel?
- Which room do you love the most and why?
- Which room do you dislike and why?
- Where and how can you make a peaceful space in your home?
- What do the colours in your home say about you?
- What five things do you feel grateful for in your home?
- Spell HOME and make each letter form a random word. Then freewrite for 10 minutes

Home is the heart of our being

Roots and your family

I see my family through the eyes of love

Your family is the first group that you belong to, and it is well documented that we learn to become from the adults around us. As children, you are directly impacted by your parent's belief systems and values. This, of course, has a profound effect on how you view your life experiences from the early stages of your life until now.

What they say has a lasting impact on our subconscious minds. For example, my dad would say *'children should be seen and not heard.'* This simple phrase says to me your opinions are unimportant, what you have to say is of no interest to me. He also said *'you can do anything you want until you get caught'* this means to me, yeah get out there and do it but be careful you will be found out as a fraud.

At some point, you will be called to deal with these patterns and beliefs that have travelled with you from childhood. In terms of balancing your root chakra, that means it is now time to deal with your family issues and trace the roots of your thinking, emotions, beliefs and behaviours.

Once you open up to healing these, it is difficult to close the lid. You will uncover beliefs about how to eat, what to say, what not to say, what to wear, jobs, voting, suitable friends and a whole host of things. As you grow, you will start to peel back the layers of family conditioning. Not all beliefs are unhealthy. Families can teach you some amazing skills.

No matter whether you can see gifts or challenges in your family relationships, they are with you for this lifetime. That doesn't necessarily mean that you will spend time with them, more that you are energetically connected.

Be grateful for what your family has provided for you and all of the lessons. Being in appreciation for what the family brings can help and support your soul's growth. Yes, there may be some awful things that have happened, no one is saying that this is any way acceptable; however, I like to think about how I have developed as a person despite the tough times. I am also profoundly grateful for the love and support of my family.

Journaling prompts

- What does family mean to you?
- What beliefs have you inherited from your family that you would now like to let go of? How can you do this?
- What sayings do you remember your family using, and how do you think these have impacted the roots of who you are?
- What are your earliest and fondest memories of your family?
- What makes your family different from other families?
- Who do you most admire and appreciate in your family? Why?
- What do you love about your family, and why?
- What do you dislike about your family and why?
- What pain has your family brought you, and how have you reframed and healed it (or how could you)?
- What lovely qualities have you inherited from your family?
- What are the most critical aspects of family life for you?
- Spell FAMILY and make each letter form a random word. Freewrite for 10 minutes

Roots and abundance

I am open to receiving all of the abundance that the Universe has to offer me

Abundance is inner wealth. It is a feeling in your heart. For example, you will feel love, peace of mind, health, wellbeing, respect, quality relationships, joy, gratitude, contentment, purpose, meaning, gratitude and appreciation for what you have.

Abundance means that there is enough for everyone, including you. Someone else's gain is not your loss because abundance means different things to different people. Being abundant is how you experience life and appreciate all of the opportunities that come your way.

The law of abundance says that there is an unlimited source of everything that you could ever need or want. However, to make this available, you have to be open to receiving it and being clear about what it is that you want. You have to open up to the flow of love and understanding what lies at the root of why you can or can't receive the abundance you desire.

By exploring abundance and what it means to you, will help you to tune into its flow and help you to become aware of what is already available to you. This will cause that vibration to expand within you, overflowing into other areas of your life.

We live in an abundant world, even though sometimes it can feel like it isn't. When you look at nature, Mother Earth is continuously providing. She knows just when to grow and when to let go. Someone with an abundant nature is kind, loving and giving; they are the kind of person you want to be around as they always help you to feel good about life. They teach us how to appreciate everything. When you are abundant, you enjoy abundance in all areas of your life.

Abundance is in everything because everything can be abundant. It's really a state of being. It is an energy which when aligned with what is right for you pours forth, both within and out into the world. To find your abundant self, you have to believe that it is possible to be an abundant person or a person with an abundant life. Abundance can be yours if you learn to first decide what it is that you want, become an open channel and then believe that it can be yours. But remember it starts on the inside and is not about getting lots of stuff, which while very nice, may not bring you happiness.

Another aspect of abundance is gratitude, being thankful for your blessings, which I hope that you have started. Practising gratitude will open you up to the natural flow of abundance. Gratitude works with the energy of the heart and helps to bring balance and harmony to you and your life. With this energy, you can enjoy more abundance in your life.

Becoming aware of your thoughts, feelings and beliefs around abundance is a wonderful starting point for creating miracles in your life. Deciding what you want and who you want to become changes your receiving energy and changes the energy around you. Once you are aligned with your desires, you need to keep your attention, focus and actions in the direction you want to go (daily aligned actions in daily magic). What you feed grows.

Abundance journaling prompts

These are your suggested journaling prompts. Use these or journal freestyle, with whatever comes up for you during the week.

- When you think of the word abundance, what is the first thing that comes to mind?
- In what ways are you already feeling abundant?
- What blocks might you have to receive abundance, and how can you reframe these?
- When you see or hear the phrase, it's better to give than receive, how do you feel that this has influenced your ability to receive abundance?
- Use this affirmation during the day - I am open to receiving all of the abundance that the Universe has to offer me, and record in your journal what happened and how you felt
- Who or what brings abundance to your life? How does that show up?

- What types of abundance do you see around you? How can you share that with others?
- How do you share the abundance in your life? How does that make you feel?
- How do you show gratitude and appreciation for the abundance you receive?
- Where do you see abundance showing up in your life?
- Where would you like to experience more abundance?
- What can you say yes to, today?
- Who will you be when you are living an abundant life?
- Spell ABUNDANCE. Describe what flowing abundance feels like?

Abundance is a process of letting go so that you can make space for what your soul wants you to have

Roots and prosperity

I am prosperous in all that I do and all that I am

In contrast to abundance, prosperity usually means the type of success that comes from having a lot of money or are wealthy. It is about wealth and success, but not necessarily from money and fame, it can also be from inner wealth and having a rich quality to your life. You can feel rich and prosperous by being satisfied with what you attract into your life and believing that you deserve all that you have and can have. Prosperity is a feeling of success, celebrating the small things and enjoying the wealth that living a rich life brings, as well as enjoying your money. So you may be living a rich life, with all of the money that you need to be able to do and have the things that you want

Feeling rich is a big part of prosperity. You can choose to feel rich no matter what you have. For some £20,000 would be a fortune, yet to someone else, it may be a days pay. But no matter which it is, it may not make either person feel prosperous. Because feeling prosperous is an attitude and a way of seeing the richness you have in your life. True wealth is spiritual prosperity. This prosperity gained through awareness and self-knowledge is like having a never-ending deposit in your cosmic bank account which you can withdraw from whenever you need it. And, your cosmic bank account is always full.

You don't have to be prosperous in order to attract prosperity. What you do need, however, is to feel that you deserve to be prosperous in order to attract it. Your feeling is the energy that attracts like energy. Shift your focus to what it feels like to live a prosperous life and have prosperity. Think about being and feeling prosperous as your relationship with the resources that you have. That can be any resources, internal and external.

Like most things in life, prosperity is about wealth beyond money and the things it can buy. It's possible to live a prosperous and abundant life even when you are earning a modest income. It's all a question of attitude and having a prosperous and abundant mindset.

Following a gratitude practice is how you create prosperity. When the Universe hears what you are grateful for you will receive more. In addition, living by your values and valuing what you have in your life, brings a level of prosperity. Add in kindness and compassion, and you will certainly be able to reap the inner rewards that come from living your life this way.

Living a life of inner richness is not about a technique or a method, it is a way of being that you decide that you want to create in your life. It is like being given a gift for you to treasure and to share where you can. Imagine feeling like you have more than enough, that you are rich in love, confidence, money, happiness, time, contentment, creativity, inner peace and whatever your heart desires

Prosperity journaling Prompts

These are your suggested journaling prompts. Use these or journal freestyle, with whatever comes up for you during the week.

- To me, prosperity and wealth mean…
- Describe your current relationship with feeling and being prosperous
- Describe the relationship you would like to have with prosperity
- What from your past is holding you back from attracting more prosperity?
- Where do you see your relationship with prosperity in 6 months? One year? Five years? Ten years?
- Where and how do prosperity and success show up for you? Where else can you harness that energy?
- To have and enjoy a prosperous life, I believe I have to…
- What do you value most in life?
- Pick five words to describe your attitude toward prosperity and being prosperous
- What is the best piece of advice you've heard about living a prosperous life?
- How prosperous would you be if you acted on your goals?

- Who will you be when you adopt a prosperous mindset?
- In what areas of your life not related to prosperity, would you like to see change or growth that might lead to more prosperity flowing your way?
- Spell PROSPERITY. Write a letter to prosperity, as if it were a person, telling him or her what kind of relationship you would like to have

Prosperity is the success that comes from following your heart

Roots and money

I am worthy of financial security

Prosperity and money can be a sticky subject for many people. Beliefs around money start forming in childhood, and these then become the roots of our money story. How your family treated money and taught you or otherwise will have an effect on your root chakra. Your family is where you first learn about money, so cast your mind back, when you were growing up, was there a lack of money, overspending, rules or sayings around money, was money controlled and used as a weapon or a reward in some way?

Was there plenty of money in the home? Was it shared freely, invested, saved, and spent wisely? What about now, how do you treat and view money and your financial health? Are you in charge of your financial health and power? Are you in debt, or have you invested wisely? These sayings all come from childhood:

- Money doesn't grow on trees
- Money doesn't buy you happiness/love
- Just be happy with what you have
- You have to work hard for your money
- Money isn't everything
- The best things in life are free
- There's no such thing as a free lunch
- Money is the root of all evil

Reflect on these sayings, I wonder which ones have left a lasting impression on you. What other ones come to mind?

The roots of your money story

Your money story is the way that you work with money. It also covers the way that you buy, sell and invest, which reveals a lot about your inner beliefs. Those beliefs come from those early childhood memories, which is why we talk about the roots of money and money with the root chakra.

Let's explore further with a couple of question:
- How wealthy you are?
- How wealthy do you feel?
- What does wealth mean to you?

When you think of wealth, are you talking about money in the bank? Or are you talking about some other kind of financial abundance? We need to remember is money is a tool, money is energy, and we're moving energy around when we're, buying, selling and investing things. Money doesn't make decisions. We do. Just pause and have a think about how wealthy you are, and what the energy of money means.

I like to look at money as financial abundance and how we have (or welcome) that abundance in our life. But often the way that we treat money means that we are hiding some underlying issues. Those really strange money patterns that we have are stopping us getting what we want and stopping us manifesting the things we want in the world. You might have patterns like, despite getting a regular income, when you get a bonus, you think, oh, I've got a bonus, and spend all of it when it might have been more helpful investing it in something else. Or you find that you thrive on challenges so are more motivated to earn money when you don't have any. You usually don't have any because when you have it, you probably squander it when you do have it.

Learning about money

Learning about money is one of the most fundamental skills for people to have. If children don't learn it early on, how are they expected to take on a money mindset later in life? It's this lack of learning that can affect the root chakra.

If you look at the profiles of financially secure people, you will find they have a different mindset than others. They know the value of money, and they know the fundamental factors of how to make their money grow. They track their money and know where it is invested. You could do this with a simple spreadsheet where you write your incomings and outgoings daily. You may also look at the lavish lifestyles of celebrities and other famous people and wish you could have the same lifestyle yourself. But, is your drive for money blinding you to what is truly important in your life?

It is often said that if you do something you love, the money will follow. There seems to be something to this because you will approach whatever you love with passion. On the other hand, if making money is your driving force, how will you accomplish that? You may chase money and find yourself getting seduced by false offers of riches. Over time, you will look back and see that not much has been accomplished.

Think about the importance of money in the context of your life. For instance, what good is having a high-paying job when you have to work 80-90 hours a week? What kind of life is that? Many people who do this, look back at their lives and wonder why they did it. While they may have a lot of money when they get older, they likely don't have anyone to share it with. Another possibility is the heavy workload to obtain that wealth gets them to an early grave. The money they earned is useless to them if that happens.

We need money, of course, we do, but if you are happy with what you are doing, money becomes a secondary priority. People do need money to live, and you shouldn't settle or work for less than you are worth. But, when you can balance a decent amount of money with doing something that you enjoy, it will bring a new level of peace satisfaction into your life.

Having a healthy money mindset that is rooted in this first chakra means that you will be better able to stay on track with your finances. A great way to do this is to have a budget. Which lets you see what money is coming in and what is going out. Think flowing root chakra energy. Obviously, you want the inflows to be more significant than the outflows and the bigger the spread, the better.

One big reason people don't budget is that they want instant gratification. We see something on television or the internet that is super cool, and we want it now. Credit cards make it easy to buy and defer payment. So when the urge to buy is strong, people justify that they have time to pay it off later.

However, do this enough, and you'll find your balances on the credit cards to be much higher than you can manage. Then you will start to feel ungrounded and unsafe, which is what we don't want.

Then there are people who make budgets but then cheat on them. They end up using all kinds of excuses as to why they spent above what the budget allowed. This is a big reason why people fail with budgets. After they cheat once, it becomes easier to do so in the future.

The key to staying on track with a budget is to focus on why you have a budget in the first place – to create healthy, secure financial roots and foundations. When you do that, you can say to yourself anytime you get the impulse to buy that it could create an imbalance in your strong roots.

Once you start to see your finances grow due and your money mindset strengthens, you will appreciate how it will motivate you to stay on track and support all other areas of your life.

Journaling prompts

- What was the money pattern in your family?
- What have you learned from your parents about money?
- What are your partner's money beliefs? (if applicable)
- Who is a breadwinner in your family? How do you feel about this term? Are you comfortable about these roles?
- Do you feel that money always eludes you? If yes, why?
- Do you often worry about not having enough money to support yourself and your family? If yes, what is the root of this fear and what is one step you can take to start to turn this around?
- Do you feel that having wealth and freedom are not meant for you? If yes, why?
- What do you think about rich people? Are you rich? In what ways?
- What do you think about the term financial freedom? Is it possible for you? If not, why not?
- Do you worry that you are not doing enough to secure your financial future? If yes, what is the root of this fear and what is one step you can take to start to turn this around?
- What do you think about other people who seem to have financial success? Do you envy them or inspired by their success?
- How are your financial needs being met? What can you do to ensure that they are always met?
- Describe your relationship with money in five words or less

- What does it mean to you to have "not enough" money?
- What does it mean to you to have "too much" money?
- What, to you, is the purpose of money?
- How do you feel about money today?
- How would you like to feel about money?
- Describe your energetic relationship with money. What would make it more joyful?
- Spell out MONEY and make each letter form a random word. Write a letter to money and abundance. Then let money and abundance write back to you

Follow your passion, find your purpose and money will follow and flow

Roots and hydration

I have a juicy life

The tree just like you needs hydrating. Your roots need water to grow to help you to have a juicy life and to create flow in your body. A tree will send its roots a long way to search for water. They make sense of the environment and know where to go to get the right ingredients to support themselves. By getting water and other nutrients, the tree can adapt and survive. The needs of the roots of a tree in nature take precedence over the leaves, for example. Which highlights the need to establish hydration for a healthy life. It will do what it can to support a juicy life.

A juicy life is available to you whenever you want it. You simply have to choose juice rather than the opposite, which is a dry life. I get that it may feel that a juicy life has passed you by, but nothing is further from the truth. Juicy is feeling rejuvenated, alive and in love with life. It's about having fun and being at one with all.

Clean, still water is essential for good health. Our bodies need water to bring in the good stuff and to flush the nasties out. When stressed and toxic, the body doesn't hydrate properly, things start to go wrong, and the cells which are the building blocks of a human essentially begin to malfunction.

When we drink water, we are looking to hydrate the smallest part of our body – the cell. Because cells, make tissues, make organs, make systems, and they make us. Start with the cell, and you will hydrate all of you.

The cells of the body are like sponges, which have to be wet to hold water. When a sponge is dry, the water falls off it. Another way to look at how water acts on dehydrated parts is to consider a dry riverbed. Where I live, it is very dry, and there's not a lot of rainfall. When it does rain, it comes down in a torrent. Because the ramblas (dried riverbeds) are hard and dry, the water cannot be absorbed and just sits on top of the hard crust. Had the riverbed been hydrated when the rains came, then the water would be absorbed.

It's, therefore, important to not just pour water in and hope that it will hydrate your cells. You have to take your time and introduce your new drinking regime so that the water does not flow straight out of you. What you notice is that when you are dehydrated and start drinking water, you will need to wee more often as you become hydrated this need to rush to the toilet will diminish.

What you will also notice as you drink more water, your body will feel grateful and reward you by giving you more energy. Water has energy. By putting water in, you can harness its power to reduce fatigue, improve your well-being and bring energy not only to your roots and foundations but to your thoughts.

Journaling prompts

- What does having a juicy life mean to you?
- What parts of your life feel a little dried out? What do you have to do to bring more juiciness into your life?
- Are you getting enough water? If not, how could you drink more?
- Staying hydrated brings more flow into your life, how can you improve the flow in your life? What would you like to flow?
- How can you be more open so that you can receive all of the juiciness that life has to offer?
- How much fun and juice can you inject into your life this week? Where will you start?
- What parts of your life are the most joyful right now?
- Where in your life do you need to make a big juicy change? What is your first step?
- Spell out JUICY and make each letter form a random word. Then freewrite for 10 minutes

Roots and being nourished

I live a nourishing life

All of the food we eat holds an energetic vibration, and for every chakra, there are foods which will support it. Having healthy hydrated roots means that you will also naturally seek out nutrients (food) that serves your body rather than destroys it. Nourishing yourself is not just about the food, it's about how often you eat the foods and eating where possible with the seasons.

As the name suggests, root foods are the ones you will tend to focus on for the root chakra. What comes to mind when you think of root foods? A root food is an edible plant that grows underground, potatoes, carrots and onions. What about sweet potatoes, ginger, garlic and one of my favourite radishes…?

Next, think about all the delicious red fruits and foods. Most red fruits and vegetables are a good source of vitamin C. Remember we said that the root chakra is connected to bone, skin, and the adrenals which all need Vitamin C to thrive.

It's also about honouring Mother Earth and nature's table. Leave packets of processed crap on the shelves. And it's about loving yourself enough to put the best fuel in you. It's about preparing it in a loving way, and it's about being mindful of where you eat, how you eat and who with.

Eating mindfully and having gratitude during your meal will support your journey. The root chakra likes connections and because there is a focus on family and belonging, enjoying meal preparation and eating with friends and family will help to strengthen it. When you are with people who love and support you, it will have a profound effect on your roots.

Nourish - is not only about what you eat, but it's also about how you nourish yourself. Think self-love and how you nourish other people. When you're looking at your diet, look at the things that aren't serving you, what can you get rid of? What can you eat that is right for you? How can you live a nourishing life? Keeping a food, energy, mood and sleep journal is eye-opening and one of the best ways to explore how and if you are nourishing yourself.

Keeping a food, energy, mood, and sleep journal

We are what we eat, ate and will eat. We are also what we think. Eating goes beyond just food. What we eat is a part of a whole system of nourishing our bodies, minds and souls.

Why keep a food, energy, mood and sleep journal?
A food journal is pretty much what you would expect. It's a tool for tracking what you eat and when to help lead you towards success with meeting your goals. They are most commonly used when supporting a weight loss or health plan.

A food, energy, mood and sleep journal additionally helps you to track other important things so that you can begin to understand you, can decide where you want to make changes and start to craft a unique plan for you. They additionally awaken you to your mental well-being, emotions, connection with your inner self and help you to notice physical symptoms which come about as a result of your lifestyle.

The benefits:
- Keeping a journal allows you to identify any not so great habits and support you to break the cycle
- Journals can help identify intolerances to certain foods. Recording what you're eating can help pinpoint foods that might be causing not so great symptoms, like bloating or something that might need further investigation
- Tracking your mood can help you reflect on how certain events might trigger changes in your emotions, allowing you to understand your inner processes better
- Tracking your energy can help you find patterns in mood, food and emotions and you may also notice how these affect your sleep
- Tracking your sleep along with everything else helps you to see where the choices you are making are having an effect on your sleep – which will affect many other things

- Food, energy, mood and sleep journals hold you accountable, which can help keep you on track regardless of what your nutrition goals are. Think about it: you're much less likely to go off course in your diet or healing plan if you know you're going to have to write it down.
- Journals are wonderful for giving you the space to express yourself and cope with your feelings
- They can ensure that you're meeting your nutritional and healing needs while getting a balanced diet. You will be able to spot things when you have a log of what you've been doing
- They can identify potential triggers that are keeping you from making changes and reaching your goals.

The bottom line is that keeping a food, energy, mood and sleep journal is a fantastic tool to help you take a closer look at your relationship with what you are eating, your energy, mood and the quality of your sleep. You'll spot how certain things make you feel and figure out what steps you can take to reach your health goals.

Finally, nourishing you is looking at all areas of your life and considering what brings you love and joy. You can nourish your soul daily with the small things that feed and energise you. Sustaining you is about putting self-care at the heart of you, which will help you to create stronger foundations. When you do this, you can live a life that has meaning.

Journaling prompts

- What does being nourished mean to you?
- What makes you feel nourished? Why? When can you enjoy more of these nourishing moments?
- How is the way in which you are digesting life affecting your ability to love and nourish yourself? How can you change this?
- How are you being your best friend? Often, we forget to treat ourselves as well as we could. What if you did?
- I feel amazing and nourished when I...
- What can you do at this moment to get yourself some nourishment, self-love and self-care?
- How are you nourishing your body so that it feels strong and can carry you through the day?
- What healthy choices can you (did you) make today because you love yourself enough to, and which will nourish your mind, body and soul?

- When will you start your food and mood journal, and what do you hope to learn from it?
- Which people nourish you and bring you joy?
- Which situations and environments nourish and why?
- Spell NOURISH and make each letter form a random word. Freewrite for 10 minutes

Roots and balance

All aspects of my life are beautifully balanced

When you are not paying attention to your inner voice, you lose equilibrium and neglect important aspects of your life. It's times like these that you lose connection with your diet and nutrition, sleep, relationships, business and connection with Mother Earth and the Universe.

When I think of balance, I see a picture of a tightrope walker making her way across the canyon, with just her inner quiet, belief and focus. Every step she takes, she moves closer to firm foundations, one false move, and she will fall out of control into the vastness and inevitable death.

Everything in life is a balancing act. The very act of eating requires a balance between the nutrients that your body needs and the quantities you consume to keep you at your optimum weight and health. Consider the potential investment in a properly planned diet to get long term returns, versus the short-term pressure to eat quickly while on the run. You know that proper nutrition is the cornerstone for keeping the systems of your body operating, but how often do you consider how the food is converted to fuel to drive each of your body's systems to ensure that nothing goes out of balance and the body remains in harmony?

- What other balances might you consider? Work-life balance or how do you balance the desire to run a growing and successful business with the needs of a growing family?
- What about the need to be always on the go with me-time?
- Giving and receiving love?
- Social commitments and quiet reflection time?

I am sure that you can think of other things right now where the balance is not as you would like it. Striking the right balance for you is knowing what is important, and creating a balanced approach to life will be different for everyone because each of you will be at different life stages with differing experiences, values, beliefs, thoughts, passions, soul purposes, diets, relationships, environments etc. Feel grateful for both what you have and what you can let go of so that you can maintain balance in your life.

Journaling prompts

- What does having a balanced life mean to you?
- How will having more balance in your life improve the quality of your life?
- How can you create more balance in your life?
- What things are you balancing and juggling? How can you bring balance back into your life?
- Where is there an imbalance, and how can you address the imbalances?
- Recall your thoughts, feelings, and physical responses to a situation that threw your off-balance, then consider what you have learned and how you can use that for increasing your potential for the future
- Spell BALANCE and make each letter form a random word. Freewrite for 10 minutes

Roots and fear

I have the courage to do anything I want

Let's talk about fear. Fear is the emotion at the root chakra. I am a great believer in having our own unique experience of things. Which means that while we can generally consider that fear typically lives in the root chakra, you may feel it at your throat chakra. This might show up in your fear to speak up. The main thing is to be aware and to be in touch with what happens for you and how you feel.

If you live in fear, you will be unbalanced and unable to create healthy foundations. Fear is looking to the future and worrying about something that you can't possibly know is going to happen. Fear is a barrier to developing your emotional intelligence and stunts your self-awareness. Which means that you will probably keep doing the same stuff, which keeps you in a holding pattern and your comfort zone.

If you search on the Internet for fear, you will see a list of names for fear of things. Just as if you search for it internally, you will find it. For me putting a label on to something gives your body permission to embed it. If you own it, in my opinion, things can only get worse. Yes, you have something to deal with, but do not own the fear beyond your initial reaction to whatever has come up. Ok, easier said than done, and I understand that.

Some people tell us that the opposite of living in or with fear is to live fearlessly, but these words don't resonate with me either. I don't like it because the fear word is part of it. Although I like the idea of being fear-less so that there is less fear. It's more how you deal with it. This is where lots of other things like faith, trust and courage, come into play. These are friends of fear.

I often wonder why if the bodies prime objective is to keep you safe, do we hurt so much and slip into fear and pain? This can be both physical and emotional pain. When my spine fractured, I felt fear ripping through every part of my being. In this case, the fear was triggered by a perceived threat. I felt threatened by osteoporosis and the medical system. I knew enough about osteoporosis as my mum has lived with it for years, and that scared me too.

I used to teach assertiveness skills, so I know intellectually that in relation to fear, there are several ways that we typically respond. One is to fight, another is to freeze, and the other is to run away. This is known as the fight, freeze or flight response.

When we sense danger, our bodies release hormones to an area of the brain called the amygdala. Depending on your response to the threat, you may experience several things. For example, you may get a racing heart or a bad tummy. What is important is that you recognise your typical response. This response is due to cortisol and adrenaline being released into the body. They, in turn, signal the adrenals (on top of your kidneys) to release the hormones we talked about. Adrenaline increases your heart rate, blood pressure and the amount of glucose (sugar) in the bloodstream. Cortisol also releases increased amounts of glucose into the bloodstream, which your brain needs to deal with the perceived threat. Glucose is food for the brain. The brain with an increased supply of food can do its work. When the fear response diminishes, everything goes back to normal.

Problems arise when you continuously live in fear. You may have heard people who are newly diagnosed with something saying that they are always tired. That's possibly because unconsciously they are fearful, and the adrenals are taking a pounding. Not only was I in pain when my spine fractured, but I was also immensely tired. My body certainly responded to all of the triggers and released all of the chemicals. Fear triggers can come at you from anywhere. The key is to be aware of what triggers you so that you can do something about them.

The other thing you may do when triggered is panic. Which is like fear escalated. Panic is normal, and it is often the first response. Think for a moment when as you are driving away from home to go on holiday and you ask, did I turn the iron off? What happens? Yes, panic. Then you calm down as you go through those final steps of closing up the house and you can see yourself doing what you always do, and the iron is off. Of course, you can ring a friend and ask them to pop in to check so that you feel reassured.

Exploring the roots of your fear

At the root chakra, we have a great opportunity to explore the roots of your fear. There is usually something that sits underneath your fear. Mine was a lack of self-love, low self-esteem and being shut down by others. You may not know what that is right now. You do not need to look for it, but know that in time it will be revealed and when it is, you can do something about it. I find that when it is revealed, there is a story typically from childhood. What is essential is to not focus on the memories, more to think about the images and key messages to look at them from 'the you' now perspective and ask what are they telling you?

Fear will attach itself to the memory of the event, and you will code and remember this memory as a time of potential unpleasantness. Then what we often do is future pace our fear, and this can lead to anxiety and stress. You start to worry about things that may never happen. Sometimes this endless worrying does bring about the event, something which is called a self-fulfilling prophecy. You may have through constant mithering have given your body permission to bring you the thing that you fear the most.

Then there is the interference. Once you feel fear, it starts to interfere with your rational and conscious thought. The knock-on effect if you let fear take control is that it can have a longer-term negative impact on your health or another area of your life. So if you have something like osteoporosis which scares you, the signals you send to your body impact your healing. All of these chemicals, while having a place in keeping us safe, are now contributing and feeding the condition we want to reverse.

So here we are on the playground of chaos. Before order, there will always be chaos. It's like our emotions trigger our systems to spiral out of order, and you find that your roots are tangled up. By exploring one thing at a time, all will be revealed. Chaos must be allowed to roam free to stir things up so that you can start to make sense of it all and make a conscious choice to take your next aligned step and untangle the mess.

Love or fear

It has been said that there is only love and fear. Everything else fits between these two things and what we are striving for is to live in the light of love. To know love is to also know fear. And while it may seem a contradiction, fear is not to be feared. It is a sign that we need to take some action. It is showing us that there is something we need and might want to do something about. Bizarrely there is great value in fear. Think about this, our bodies use fear to get us out of danger fast. That has to be great, but you wouldn't want to be on high alert all of the time, would you?

When you stand on any part of the love fear spectrum, it is a call for you to take a step closer to love. Imagine if at one end is a dark tunnel or circle and at the other is a heart. The call is to move closer to the heart. This is your home. At your heart, you make a connection with you, make a connection to other's hearts, to the heart of Mother Earth and with the heart of consciousness. Ask yourself:

- Is your what you want for your life created from love or fear?
- Are you:
  - Going towards something?
  - Running away from something?
- What would happen if I went with love?
- Who will I be if I embrace living in love?

Find your emotional flow

As you go through the Venus gateway or you experience something in life, you may be presented with an emotion to deal with. While the primary emotion of the root chakra is fear, you may travel from fear to guilt then lies, illusion and then back to fear. Remember we touched on patterns in the chapter on the Venus gateway?

When this happens, follow the flow of the emotions through the chakras and explore how each one is impacting you, what you need to know, what might be blocking you and what you need to let go of. You can use your hands to ask each in turn what that chakra wants you to know. It will never just be as simple as just being fear or just guilt. It all starts with a root cause which impacts the next one and the next one.

Root causes are often not that simple to discover, so what we do as the day progresses is to allow images, words, memories, sounds, songs, feelings etc. to come to us. There will be clues in all of these. Record them in your journal, rather than trying to over analyse what they mean. As you work with the

Venus gateway and your chakras, you will learn more about you and what the root of what ails you is. And then you can heal, grow and find your flow.

When you have gone through this process, consider how to forgive each of these parts of you (see the next chapter on letting go). By releasing and letting go, you will bring more inner peace and contentment into your life.

Journal it: Ground and centre with the three hearts meditation. Recall a recent fearful experience, freewrite about the experience for 10 minutes. When you read back through the journal entry, what do you notice about your patterns and the flow of your emotions?

Ways to overcome fear and break through your comfort zone

Of course, we know that we are not the only person on earth that has fears. Even people with powerful and important positions have fears. Every person who must learn something new experiences fear and discomfort before they have a breakthrough. It's totally a normal part of human existence, and you're no different.

Define the fear and the effects it has on you

When you start to experience feelings that you identify as a fear that feels like it might stop you from achieving your desires, take the time to stop what you're doing and focus for a moment on what you are really feeling.

For example, if you're trying to learn something new, but you're feeling frustrated and confused because you don't feel as if you know what you're doing, you could allow the fear of thinking you can't learn it to stop you. Instead, take a break to identify the emotions you're feeling and how it's affecting your body. Instead, reframe and turn your cannots into cans.

Journal it: Try this now, find something that you think you can't do because you are fearful. Write I can't and what you feel about it. Then write I can, add in who will I be when I can do this thing?

Understand your trigger

One way to overcome fear is to recognise your fear trigger, make a note of what happened in the lead-up. Ask what the trigger is, it may not be what you currently think it is. Make a note of your physical state and emotions, what you saw, felt or heard. What do you learn about yourself from this? Is there a pattern, e.g. fear (roots), to guilt (sacral) to lies (throat)?

Ask yourself the right questions

When you first feel fear, especially if you are afraid that fear is going to block you from success, ask the right questions. The right questions are almost always:

- What is the worst thing that could happen?
- What is the best thing that could happen?

When you define the very worst thing that can happen if you do or don't do the thing that is causing you the fear, it can help push you forward. And the reframing question is a great follow up.

Journal it: What do you feel fear around? Explore and ask the two questions above. What do you learn?

Accept your fear

Now that you know what the fear is doing to your mind and body take the time to accept it. This fear is normal and part of your learning process. It's just your mind's way of pushing back a little to keep you safe as you gain a better understanding. Write down what can happen realistically so that you know that learning this new thing is not actually going to harm you in any way. Use the questions in the previous point.

Change your perspective and reframe

Fear is often what stops us changing. One way to learn to face your fears is to write them down and then create dialogue around them. If you feel especially stuck, sometimes looking at solutions from a new perspective can help. Ask someone who has done it before to help you. Read books, blog posts and watch YouTube videos to learn whatever you need to know to help you look at the situation in a new way. I also want to ask if you have a crystal ball? Can you see into the future and know, absolutely know that you will fail or whatever is coming up for you? Fear can be translated into false evidence appearing real.

Reframing fear is powerful and will help you to change how you feel, the triggers and any associated emotions and behaviours. What you may not know is that fear and excitement trigger similar responses. One can be unpleasant, and one isn't. They are both drivers for change. It is up to us to make conscious choices. One thing that always works for me is to use the word fear and find another meaning. As an example

- F - Feeling fabulous when in FLOW
- E - Excitement
- A - Acceptance
- R – Release

    Or

- F - Faith
- E - Excitement
- A - Acceptance
- R - Resilience

Journal it: Have a go while you focus on your situation. It's quite fascinating what comes out when you look at fear this way. It makes it easier to surrender and let go of fear.

Write about your fears

This is undoubtedly a time when your journal is one of your best friends. Think about this, if you write about your fears they are almost certainly halved as you share the energy of that vibration with the page and therefore start to dissipate that feeling. When you write about overcoming difficult obstacles, you are sharing hope with your heart. When you write about success and celebration, you have a friend to share that with.

- What are you afraid of?
- How has that fear manifested?

- What is this fear really telling or showing me?
- How can you reframe this fear?
- What lies at the root?
- Who would I be if I didn't feel this fear?

Be mindful of your thoughts

The truth is, you are so much more powerful than you realize. Your thoughts really do control your emotions. It might seem like your emotions are controlling your thoughts, but that's not true. You are in full control over your thoughts even if you don't believe that yet. Learn how to identify and reverse negative beliefs and replace them with positive or at least neutral thoughts to help reduce fear. Write these in your journal. What do you learn?

Ask for support

Feelings of anxiety and fear often elicit thoughts about "going slightly crazy.". Some of your thoughts could increase your anxiety and fear. Again, if you need support, ask. Never be alone with these thoughts.

Understand the power of now

If everyone on the earth realized the power of now, we'd be further along our evolutionary journey. Yesterday is gone and cannot be changed, tomorrow is not guaranteed, all you really have is right now. The more you can use this knowledge for yourself, the more likely you are to overcome your fears and breathe through your comfort zone.

What my future self knows

Go to a future version of you and ask them any burning questions you have, knowing that you already know the answer. There is no such thing as a wrong decision or wrong answer. When you consider what you choose as the way forward, ask are you choosing from love or fear? Then ask what the next right step is? Make sure you are connected with the energy of it already being done and then making decisions from that version of you. What do you need to get you to where you need to be?

Visualise what's next

Sometimes when you're experiencing fear about something, it helps to visualise what is next. By that, I mean is asking yourself what the next aligned next step is? Let's assume you're fearful due to a presentation you're giving in front of 1000 people. You have identified your rapid heartbeat, feelings of nausea and the hot flash that's coming on as fear of public speaking.

Instead of focusing on fear, focus on what happens next. See in your mind what happens if you don't do the speech. See in your mind what happens if you do it. What happens if you make a mistake? As you visualize, you can help reduce fear by focusing on what happens next realistically.

Journal it: Look through the various ideas and explore the roots of your fear and then consider how to reframe in a way that works for you.

Journaling prompts

- One thing that makes me feel nervous or scared:
- When this fear is triggered, what thoughts go through your mind?
- In what areas of the body do you feel the fear?
- How does your body react (forehead sweat, sticky palms, etc.)?
- How do you respond to this fear (fight / flight / avoidance / feel depressed / etc.)?
- What exactly is it that makes you fearful? Dig deep to the source and be specific
- Realistically, what are the chances of this happening?
- What can you do to lessen the likelihood of it happening?
- What's the worst that could happen if your fear comes to fruition?
- What is the long-term cost (emotional, physical, financial, etc.) of not overcoming this fear?
- If the worst-case scenario happened, how would you consciously work through it? What steps would you take?
  - What benefits will you receive if you work through this fear?

Fear is excitement in disguise

Roots and letting go

Letting go is easy

I believe that we can use letting go to create change, which means if we can get rid of the toxins in our life, it can help us to heal, improve communications and find that all-important inner peace. Letting go also creates space for something more beautiful to enter your life.

There is so much that we can let go of to create space, better energy and healthier roots. What about letting go of the rubbish that your body doesn't need, getting rid of people in our life and getting rid of other rubbish in your home and environment.

We have already looked at and discussed decluttering your home. If you were to look around your house, what stuff could you give to charity? Or what stuff could you sell on eBay? What about who is in your life that are not good people for you? I know it's difficult to get rid of people from your life but think about how you can spend more time with the people that nourish you. We talk reason season, lifetime people. Who is in your life for a reason, a season or a lifetime? Who are those people that you want to hold on to, and the people that you don't want because they're toxic?

Letting go doesn't mean just dumping stuff or washing your hands of something or someone, it means forgiving and letting go of your attachment to something or someone so that you can release them, and heal yourself.

Forgive your blocks - let them go

Forgive means to let go. It doesn't mean to forget or to condone your actions or the actions of others. It is a powerful opportunity to declutter your stuff and let go of the past. It means that you can open a space to the beautiful soul that resides within you. In the shadow of not forgiving lies fear, guilt and shame. In the light is inner peace and contentment.

We all have blocks. No matter how much life decluttering that you have done, something will pop up. This is a great opportunity to make a list of all of the perceived blocks you may have when you think about what you want. And to do this regularly. You could list your blocks in the categories of your life focus areas. This will prove interesting as it could point a particular chakra or period that you may have found challenging. Steps in decluttering blocks are:

- Make a list of your blocks, no matter how big or small
- Affirm that you are ready to let go of what does not serve you
- Notice what memories come up and what they teach you - what are the messages - the key is not to dwell, more to acknowledge and get ready to forgive and let go

Then forgive them with Ho'oponopono – to make right. Which is made up of four seemingly simple statements:

- I'm sorry
- Please forgive me
- Thank you
- I love you

The combination of remorse, forgiveness, gratitude and love is powerful. The power is in the feeling, the energy you release to the Universe, remembering that like energy attracts like energy. You can say these in any order - so don't worry that you have to memorise them. You do not have to complete the whole list in one go. Choose what feels right and do these. Notice what comes up for you, write and release in your journal.

The roots of letting go

When you consider the roots of your emotions or feelings, what do you need to let go of? How would you feel if you did and who would be if you traced the roots of your pain and reframed? Holding on to stuff causes pain. It also creates dis-ease in the body as your emotions manifest into something unpleasant. As you let go and release your 'stuff' you can create more ease in your body and therefore your life.

Letting go of these old beliefs and patterns of behaviour that do not serve you will support healthy roots. At the root, there will be emotions to let go of, such as fear and anger. These emotions, when out of balance, tell us that we have become detached from our foundations. Fear may be telling you that you have lost trust in your life's path or have lost your way. Noticing these out of balance emotions are an invitation from your soul to examine the structure and environment that you have created which may not be serving you. Consider what these are doing to your life, bring yourself back to the present and work on soothing and nourishing yourself so that you come back into balance.

Letting go (and forgiving) will improve your physical health, which is fundamental to your life and all of your energy systems. Without your physical health, your energy will be low. When you feel sluggish, you won't make the best conscious choices. You might be tempted to live on caffeine or sugary foods, but after the temporary high, you will crash and begin to feel stressed.

All living things carry a specific energy frequency or vibration. Let's go back to the trees. Trees are not just roots, they also have a trunk, branches, leaves, fruit, berries and nuts. Trees play a significant role in circulating energy and contributing to the health of the planet. You, like a tree, will not survive well if your environment is under attack. A certain amount of stress helps us to adapt to our environment, however too much, triggers a chronic stress response. Having too much stress in your life will suck the energy right out of you.

In his book The Biology of Belief, Bruce Lipton talks about how your thoughts affect your cells. If we are living in a perpetually stressed place, imagine what kind of thoughts are being passed to your cells. They will respond in the best way that they know how to.

Inside of each of these cells, which are listening in all the time is an old set of programs called unexpressed emotions. Every stressful moment and corresponding thought hangs around doing damage, and we don't even realise it. Think of a computer which is constantly under attack from viruses and other unwanted gremlins. I see my journal as an anti-virus program. Where the past grunge can be gouged out and a pathway to understanding carved instead. Words are powerful, and as we let go of these unexpressed emotions and realise who we are, why those repeating patterns of how our lives became so fractured, our cells start to respond in kind. There is more to it than that, but stress and emotions are a great place to begin to understand how your body responds to life and the amount of available energy you have.

Imagine losing these attachments, becoming aware of why you do what you do, and how practising gratitude and being mindful can help you to create new beautiful root systems that will serve you more effectively and give you more energy.

The energy of the root chakra forms the foundation and support for energy to be able to flow and align the rest of your chakras. It's essential to look after all of your energy points, and as your life changes, as the world spins, your energy will change. It's important to take the time to check-in at your roots first and let the energy flow throughout the rest of your body.

It seems that life is rarely straightforward, that we have lots of lessons to learn, but which are also gifts. Every day something crops up, and yet another layer needs peeling away. I often have a good cry when something comes to bite me on the bottom. What, I ask, is this new thing you want me to deal with? Why me and why now? Why not me and why not now? Now is as good as time as any to deal with whatever it is and get it out of my life.

Letting go creates space for more opportunities and possibilities, and who doesn't want more of that? Learn to embrace and love letting go. It is good for the soul and creates freedom. All you have to do is to decide to let go.

Journaling prompts

- What does letting go mean to you?
- The words letting go make you think… and make you feel…
- When I am finally able to let go of the most difficult thing, person, place, or situation, I will feel…
- Today, I choose to let go of the things I can't control, including…

- When you think of where you are, what or who do you need to forgive or let go of so that you make space for new opportunities?
- What physical clutter that needs letting go of has been complicating your life and diverting you from meaningful life experiences? How can you sort this out?
- What mental or emotional clutter that needs letting go of has been complicating your life and diverting you from meaningful life experiences? How can you sort this out?
- Who needs to leave your life?
- What three habits do you need to let go off and what are the first steps you need to take?
- What's not working? How will it feel to let these things go?
- What is working because you have let something go, and can you have more of these things?
- Take a moment to think about when you've felt most mentally alive and had lots of energy. Where were you? Who were you with? What were you doing?
- When you have let go of what does not serve you, how can you bring more energy into your day and life?
- What drains your energy, that needs letting go of and how can you reframe and refocus?
- Who drains your energy that needs letting go of, and how can you protect yourself?
- If you let go and trust, what might happen is…?
- When you trace the roots of what you are holding onto, what do you discover? What do you learn that means that you can now choose to make some changes?
- Spell out LETTING GO and make each letter form a random word. Write a letter to letting go

When I let go and open my heart, I make space for the wonder of creation

The roots of your successful life

I am connected to the roots of my success

The roots of success is another way to look at your bucket list and determine how you want to grow the things that you desire. Review your bucket list and intuitively choose the one thing that you want to work on right now, You are going to write your desire into the roots of the tree overleaf. If you want to draw your own tree with roots, please do.

Around your desire, focus on the roots of why you want this thing. For example, I have always wanted to write creatively and felt that I have never been allowed or encouraged to express myself this way. Now that my fear is going I feel more confident about doing it. I was also too scared to read my work out, and now I feel more comfortable and at ease with critiquing.

Next, take your attention to the branches, on the right:

- Write all of the benefits you will get when you have your desire
- How you will feel?
- Who will you be?

And finally, on the left:

- Write ten things that you can do to make it happen
- Pick one that you can implement right away and do it

The roots of my success flow from the abundance of joy in my heart

Prescription for healthy roots

My roots are healthy, wealthy, healed and happy

Practice grounding

Grounding simply means connecting yourself to a source of earthing energy. Which means plugging yourself into something that helps you to feel connected to Mother Earth and safe in who you are and where you are. Grounding also means discharging excess energy by being in the moment. There are lots of ways of doing this.

Three hearts meditation

I do this with the three hearts meditation, which I have repeated here for ease. Imagine that roots are growing from your feet into the heart of Mother Earth. Place your hands on your heart. Take your awareness to your heart. Take your breath from your heart down through your roots and into the heart of Mother Earth. Breathe in and out a few times. Next, take your awareness from your heart up and out through your crown chakra and connect to the heart of consciousness. Breath in and out of your heart into the heart of consciousness a few times. Then imagine that there is a golden thread connecting the heart of consciousness to your heart and the heart of Mother Earth. When you are ready, take a few deep breaths and stretch.

Create an anchor

I use my fingers for this. I'll choose four words, the first represents the worse feeling and the last where I want to get to, which a less emotional state. When I feel that I need to ground and come back to the centre, I press each finger in turn while focusing on my breath. Another way is to imagine roots growing from your feet and sinking into the heart of Mother Earth. Eating something comforting, putting your wrists under cold running water, taking a short walk are also helpful. You could try stopping where you are and looking around you and counting three things that you can see which are a particular colour, listening for two sounds, and noticing one smell.

Get out in nature and be more active

Getting active will give you greater stamina, stronger muscles, lower your risk of diabetes, heart disease and stroke, a lower risk of osteoporosis (brittle bones), improve mood, posture and give you a better shape and appearance, for example.

Living an active lifestyle can also help you to feel more energetic and feel better about yourself by giving you more confidence. You will also feel more relaxed, sleep better, and be able to deal with everyday stresses more effectively, reducing your risk of depression.

One of the easiest ways to have an active lifestyle is to get out in nature and walk. Connecting with Mother Earth is grounding. The Earth is where we get the beautifully vibrant, abundant colours of red, brown and black. When I feel ungrounded, or my head is in the clouds, I go out for a walk with the dogs. Hearing my feet on the ground brings me back to Earth and feeling more settled.

It is when I am outside, I can reflect on these obtrusive thoughts, consider the facts, to make sense of things I cannot change, how to accept what I cannot change and how to reframe the way I see things. This helps me to feel centred.

Being outside means that you are in the sunshine (well, I guess that depends on where you live...). The sun is essential to your growth and is one of the most essential sources of energy. Vitamin D is produced naturally in the body by the sun. The sun boosts the immune system, eases depression, makes you feel great, and it's a vital vitamin for the bones (your foundation). More importantly, of course, without the sunlight, there would be no life on earth.

One way to ground is to walk in the woods, sit with your back to the trunk or do as I do and simply place my hands on the trunk and connect. When I am surrounded by trees or touching a tree, the essence of the tree communicates a feeling of security, stability, and safety. Because trees are so firmly anchored to the Earth, they are great teachers of grounding.

To feed your soul, remember to get out in nature often and appreciate all that Mother Nature is offering you. Make a plan to be outside and enjoy the peace in nature. Here's a few questions for reflection:

- Where will you go?
- What will you do when you get there?
- What do you enjoy most about being out in nature?
- Where is your favourite outside space, and how does it make you feel when you are there?
- Imagine you are in your favourite outside space, what can you hear, see, smell and touch?

Focus on your breathing

Try some of the breathing exercises in the alchemy of the breath and stay being mindful of your breath. Keep noticing your in-breath, your out-breath and feel the breath soothing you, comforting you and nurturing you. Feel the inner peace that this brings. Now surrender. Keep breathing, noticing your in-breath and your out-breath…

Choose a root chakra area to focus on

One of the things that will help you to create healthy roots is to pick one of the prompts areas and spend a week focusing on the questions, being grateful and designing specific affirmations. At the end of the week, reflect on what you learn about yourself in this area.

Declutter

Think about your physical space and environment and take some time each week to declutter different areas. Perhaps pick a room and time yourself for 15 minutes – what can you declutter in that time?

Nourish yourself

Look after your diet. Add healing foods to your diet and look for foods that support the root chakra. Think root vegetables, red foods and anything that makes you feel soothed.

Create some structure in your life

The root chakra loves a bit of structure. Think about how you can create a filing system, sort out your bookshelf or case, clean out your junk drawer and sort out your finances by doing your accounts. Journaling every day is creating structure.

Focus on abundance

Have you ever considered just how lucky you are? Of course, everyone has things that feel outside of their control. Sometimes it can feel like there is never enough of anything - time, money, resources, and health. Take a moment to think about the things you do have. List them, no matter how small. Consider that if even you don't have everything you'd like, you do have things to be thankful for. Find the abundance in your life and celebrate it. This is where you will find true fulfilment and happiness. Even in your darkest moments, you always have something worth celebrating. You are richer than you think. When you focus on what I call wealth beyond money, things you are grateful for you are creating an abundance mindset.

Reflective practice and reflection

The power of reflection will change your life.

Reflection is your response to experiences, situations, events or new information and a phase where processing and learning can take place. When you reflect your unconscious mind searches for evidence and analyses it. After which it tries to make meaning and draw conclusions based on the evidence presented. Once you have been able to evaluate what you are reflecting on, you can then decide what's next. Reflection is a powerful learning experience, which is not about sitting in the lotus position omming, though of course, you could. Reflection has a few basic elements: -

- **Retelling**- state the basic facts (write a journal entry) and consider how you felt about it at the time and how you feel about it now
- **Examine** – examine and relate the feelings or events to other times when you have felt the same way
- **Reflecting** – How do you change your behaviours? What possible alternatives, perspectives, meanings, or links can you see?

Reflection, then allows you to further process what you have written so that you can make meaning of your words, make changes, and start the healing process. Reflection is simply a process which enables you to make meaning from your writing, challenge your thinking, learn who you are and gives you the opportunity to make choices about changing the way you behave.

To make sense of your writing, you simply have to leave it. Reflective thinking is about going back and looking at your journal, analysing what you have written, with the goal of making decisions about what to do or what not to do. It is when you do this that you will discover inspiration and clarity.

You can reflect on what you have written at any time. When you come to reflect on your journaling after you have completed all of these prompts, consider how what you have written about has impacted your life, ask these questions.

- What have you learned about you?
- What are your most significant insights?
- What is one thing that you will do differently because of what you have learned?

Focus your reflections on creating healthy roots and foundations. Before you start to reflect and write, read through your journal so far, and simply become aware of anything that stands out for you. If you have used the mandalas focus on the colours that you have chosen, what do you learn from these colours?

Simple reflection

Simple reflection comes from taking any of your journal entries and completing the following questions.
- Describe the situation
- What did I do? What happened? What did I say?
- Who was with me?
- How well or not so well did it go?
- How do I think or feel about it?
- What did I think about but not say?
- What did I learn?
- What will I do differently next time?
- How will I do it differently next time?
- What have I achieved?

- What have I learnt about myself?

Silence as a stimulus for action

In the spaces and the silence come the answers. Close your eyes and breathe into the silence. In the silence, further information, memories, ideas, solutions and ways forward will come. It is in the allowing, the silence, the void and nothingness that we find our deepest well of resources.

Learning to stand back and being out of the picture

Sometimes when you write about painful experiences, you start to relive the experience, which may be unhelpful. It is vital to get this stuff out and on to paper. Once we have done that, it is even more important that, when we reflect on it, we do so from a stand back position and to remain out of the picture, so that we can view it objectively and without emotion.

We take a stand back / out of the picture position so that it protects it from the pain we may have been feeling, it separates feeling from the images that we can see, it allows us to see the event in a new way and therefore put it to bed.

Out of the picture reflection

- Take one of your journal entries and write it on a piece of paper
- Place the paper on the floor
- Standing looking at the paper and journal entry, reflect on the situation
- Look at it from a distance and think about how you might resolve it or change it

In the picture

When we reflect on something that was great, it is better to reflect when we are in the picture so that we can remember, see, feel and hear all the great things that happened. You can use these positive experiences whenever you are feeling down.

In the picture reflection

- Take one of your journal entries and write it on a piece of paper. This needs to be about something good and positive
- Place the paper on the floor
- Standing on the paper and journal entry, reflect on the situation
- Close your eyes. Let all the great feelings wash over you

NB: In some cultures, standing on paper is a no-no. In which case, place the paper to your heart or use your intuition to know where to put it.

The power of I statements

Use "I" statements. Review and look for journal entries that say things like 'he/she made me....'. You are looking to change the 'he made me', to, 'I felt' or 'I did or said'.

- For example, he /she made me so mad when I walked through the door and saw the pile of dishes, once again piled up, and he/she was sitting on the sofa drinking tea.
- Could be changed to I felt so angry when....

After which you can examine why it made you angry and what has to happen to change your feelings. You are looking at how you can take ownership of your feelings and reactions.

The power of your language

If you listen to your voice on a recording it doesn't sound like you, what we hear is the sound resonating inside us, the person we are talking to hears a different sound, because it is travelling to them in another way. When you read your journal back, it may not seem like you too. This is because it is your heart and soul speaking through your pen as a channel.

When people talk about voice, you usually think of the noise that comes out of your mouth, and of course, in part it is. When someone speaks to you, what do you get a sense of?

- The person

- Pitch and tone
- Understanding
- Emotion
- Passion
- Purpose
- Something else?
- Do you paint a picture in your head, hear sounds, get a feeling or a sense of all of those – what happens for you?

The voice is a fantastic instrument, and I, for one moment, couldn't begin to tell you how it all works. For a short period, I was having singing lessons so that I could be a better thinker and speaker. I was amazed by how my voice resonated in different parts of my body, sometimes in my stomach and sometimes bouncing around my skull. I tried to follow it, to understand what it was doing and why. I was encouraged to practise scales and make funny noises with my lips and tongue in strange positions. What amazed me was that I let go of fear and gave it a go. When you read your journal entries back, let go and see what comes back to you. It's your voice. Journaling has a lot to do with finding your voice and speaking your truth.

What do you notice about your written language? Words shape people and behaviours. Language is one of our tools for expression and communication. When you use reflective practice and study how you use language – what words and phrases you unconsciously choose and combine it will help you to better understand yourself and why you behave the way you do. Language plays a significant role in how you and others perceive the world. As you read your writing, you will discover what words and phrases influence you, unknowingly. Again, ask, what do you learn?

Reflections, feedback & follow up

When it's time to reflect, picture yourself as a tree with your roots connecting you to the earth. This is how you will stay connected, grounded and secure. Drink in the energy of Mother Earth up into your heart, see yourself creating a strong, energetic foundation for your life's journey. Imagine energy flowing from Mother Earth and holding you secure and in your power. This establishes a stable place in the world for you. When you are ready, go with the flow, and put pen to paper. Colouring in a mandala before you reflect is also a fantastic way to take your reflection practice deeper. When you reflect, you are looking for linkages, patterns, pictures, common points of reference and aha moments. Images and emotions stored in your long-term memory will come to mind to help. For me, it is a combination of logic and creativity. When you are ready, reflect and see how far you have grown.

Question time

Journal it: Answer these questions:

- What went well? Why?
- What needs letting go of or stopping? Why?
- What needs starting? Why?
- Look back over your journal and pick 5 things you are most grateful for
- What good things happened?
- What were your favourite moments?
- What do you want to celebrate?
- Who has taught you something important? How does this make you feel?
- Who are you most grateful to?
- How can you appreciate what you have in your life more?
- What is your most important goal, desire or intention for going forward?
- What habits do you need to change?
- How healthy are your roots and foundations?
- Who are you now that you have come on this journey?

Learn more about Dale

Dale discovered the power of journaling and writing early on in life and has used it as she describes 'to save her life' many times. By putting pen to paper, connecting with her muse and combining that with reflective practice, Dale has been able to change her perspective in her journey to meet a better version of herself.

In 2018, her spine fractured. One of the first things that she did was grab a new journal and begin to explore why and how to heal osteoporosis naturally. She used her journal to pour out her fear, confusion and overwhelm. She used it for research into ways that nutrition could help her to rebuild her bones, life and energy. In her darkest moments, she screamed at the pages which held her words and eventually she found peace. She knows first-hand the power of journaling and shares with you, how you can use it to also 'save your life.'

Dale also called upon the healing power and wisdom of her chakras and worked with crystals to use energy to support the healing process. She'd learned about energy medicine in her early 30's and was grateful for the knowledge in this time of need. Today like journaling, Dale works with her chakras and crystals daily.

You can discover more at - www.daledarley.com

Do you want more journaling prompts? Sign up for 101 days for being me.

https://daledarley.com/101-days-of-being-me/

Check out her courses - https://daledarley.com/workshops-courses/

Free book resources are here - https://daledarley.com/love-to-journal-resources/

Actions:

- Venus gateway
- daily journey
- Sun reflect on ask
- End month reflect.

Printed in Great Britain
by Amazon